LAST STAND
of the
RED SPRUCE

About Island Press

Island Press, a nonprofit organization, publishes, markets, and distributes the most advanced thinking on the conservation of our natural resources—books about soil, land, water, forests, wildlife, and hazardous and toxic wastes. These books are practical tools used by public officials, business and industry leaders, natural resource managers, and concerned citizens working to solve both local and global resource problems.

Founded in 1978, Island Press reorganized in 1984 to meet the increasing demand for substantive books on all resource-related issues. Island Press publishes and distributes under its own imprint and offers these services to other nonprofit organizations.

Funding to support Island Press is provided by The Mary Reynolds Babcock Foundation, The Ford Foundation, The George Gund Foundation, The William and Flora Hewlett Foundation, The Joyce Foundation, The Andrew W. Mellon Foundation, Northwest Area Foundation, The J. N. Pew, Jr. Charitable Trust, Rockefeller Brothers Fund, and The Tides Foundation.

About the Natural Resources Defense Council

The Natural Resources Defense Council, Inc. (NRDC) is a nonprofit membership organization dedicated to protecting America's natural resources and to improving the quality of the human environment. With offices in New York City, Washington, D.C. and San Francisco, CA, and a full-time staff of lawyers, scientists and environmental specialists, NRDC combines legal action, scientific research, and citizen education in a highly effective environmental protection program.

NRDC's major accomplishments have been in the areas of energy policy and nuclear safety; toxic substances; air and water pollution; urban transportation; natural resources and conservation; and the international environment. NRDC has approximately 65,000 members and is supported by tax-deductible contributions.

LAST STAND of the RED SPRUCE

Robert A. Mello

Introduction by

Senator Patrick J. Leahy

Washington, D.C. ☐ Covelo, California

Library of Congress Cataloging-in-Publication Data

Mello, Robert A., 1946–
Last stand of the red spruce.

Bibliography: p.
Includes index.
1. Red spruce decline—Vermont—Green Mountains. 2. Plants, Effect of acid precipitation on—Vermont—Green Mountains. 3. Red spruce—Vermont—Green Mountains—Ecology. 4. Forest ecology—Vermont—Green Mountains.
I. Title
SB608.R33M45 1987 363.7'386 87-82039
ISBN 0-933280-37-8 (pbk.)

Manufactured in the United States of America

10 9 8 7 6 5 4 3 2

To
Becky and Kim

Contents

List of Figures

Introduction

"Acid Rain."

This now familiar term was first etched into our collective conscience years ago. We have since become so familiar with it that most of us believe we understand the full extent of its destructive qualities.

Unfortunately, we are discovering that the acid rain hit-list is expanding. Robert Mello's book tells us that we must now add new casualties to the deaths of lakes and rivers—thousands and thousands of trees, entire forests, are succumbing to the adverse effects of acid rain.

I see it most clearly in the beautiful Green Mountains of Vermont, the mountains which give my state its name. Each year, as I look out my window to the forest covering Camels Hump, I see the steady browning of what was once an all-green forest.

This phenomenon began shortly after World War II as the red spruce in Vermont began to turn brown and die in increasing numbers. In recent years, we have seen this decline rapidly accelerate.

By most accounts, acid rain appears to be the culprit in the steady decline of the red spruce. Mr. Mello's well-documented, engrossing book adds ammunition to the arsenal of those advocating control of acid rain. He weaves an immensely readable account that is part detective story, part history, part science and part rallying cry.

Last Stand of the Red Spruce makes a strong call for reducing acid rain emissions and establishes the need for immediate action. In his clear and concise style, Mr. Mello makes it plain that the time has come to go beyond waiting for a technological fix.

There was cause enough years ago to enact legislation cutting pollution emissions to levels compatible with human health and the future of our lands and forests.

Now, as we consider this problem again in the 100th Congress, the issue is at a critical juncture. Robert Mello has added an eloquent new voice to the chorus calling for immediate action in the fight against acid rain.

Senator Patrick J. Leahy
July, 1987

Foreword

That hideous verbal and meteorological concoction "acid rain" entered our vocabulary and atmosphere so many years ago that it runs the risk of being treated as an inevitable fact of life; part of the aerial landscape, as it were. We all know about the acidic fallout from power plants and industrial pollution contaminating rivers and lakes and producing an annual political squabble between Canada and the Reagan administration. We know that fish die in huge numbers and billion of dollars are lost in damage to our buildings, cars and monuments.

Last Stand of the Red Spruce changes the picture by forcing some new and disturbing concepts into our notion of the consequences of allowing acid rain to fall unchecked across our land. We must consider the possible disappearance of whole forests of our favorite and most valuable evergreens.

Concern about the effects of air pollution on forests has been with us for a long time. In this book, Robert Mello describes the scientific debate about forest death, or *Waldsterben* as the Germans call it, with unique clarity. He then arrives at the common sense and inescapable conclusion that we must stop spewing sulfur dioxide and other chemical pollutants into the air, or the forests will surely suffer the consequences.

Like many of his neighbors, Robert Mello, a Vermont attorney, and, as you shall soon learn, a first class investigative reporter as well, was troubled by the declining conditions of the beautiful and valuable red spruce forests which wreath the Appalachian Mountains from North Carolina to Maine and into Canada.

The raw elements of nature—sun and sky, rock and rain—make the Green Mountains of Vermont a place of unique beauty and a haven for people with a special concern for their environment. The ruggedness of Vermont's mountain peaks can disguise the delicacy of nature's balance. Near the top of those mountains the soil is not rich, the climate is very harsh, only certain kinds of trees can survive and to do so they must have exactly the right conditions or they give way to the many natural foes they face—parasites, fungi and fire.

The red spruce began to die in Vermont during the 1950s. But Vermont is not alone in witnessing the suffering of these graceful trees. All of New England and Canada and states as far south as Georgia are experiencing the same loss.

Mello took time off from his law practice to make a serious investigation of the situation. His inquiries led him to other researchers who have been studying the same question. Here then is the story of the New England scientists who began by asking why the trees are dying, and then determined that a principal cause is acid rain from air pollution.

The author has a rare knack, the ability to translate technical information and scientific jargon into plain language without distorting the meaning or condescending to his reader. The result is a treatise which states its case with both accuracy and passion.

Last Stand of the Red Spruce presents a vivid portrayal of what motivates the advocates of acid rain control. The message in this book will help us win the battle in Congress, where acid rain control legislation has been bottled up for many years.

That struggle is now entering what may be a decisive phase. Here is how my colleague at the Natural Resources Defense Council (NRDC), attorney David Hawkins, recently described to a Congressional panel the history of efforts to win acid rain control: "Since 1980 opponents of acid rain control have trotted out a series of arguments against a new law—there is no problem; we don't understand the cause of the problem; we don't know how to fix the problem or we can't afford to do it. As the weaknesses of these arguments have been exposed, control opponents have turned to what is traditionally the last weapon in their arsenal of delay—they predict a vastly superior solution to the problem just over the horizon, and urge Congress to wait until it arrives.''

That is roughly where the battle lines are drawn as this book goes to the printers. The argument that we must wait for better control methods is not a new one. Essentially the same argument was made twenty years ago by the same industries that are now most vigorously opposing acid rain controls. Then, as now, the issue was: Should the federal government require a major reduction in emissions from the electric utilities and other major industries? The utility and coal industries argued then for delay and promoted taller smoke stacks as the solution that would buy the time required to carry out the research that could one day give still better solutions. In 1967, the coal industry was telling Congress that the emerging technology of flue gas desulfurization (FGD) would be a method that could, with three to five years of additional development, be used to attack the coal sulfur problem.

These systems, scrubbers as they are usually called, and other methods were developed and improved through the 1970s and are now proven reliable means of controlling emissions from both new and existing power plants. However, now that we have been through two decades of research and development and refinement of these and other control systems, these emerging technologies of twenty years ago are decried by their erstwhile boosters, and our attention is once more directed to methods that have not yet arrived.

Meanwhile, in West Germany, where *Waldsterben* has long been a national concern, an acid rain control program is now being implemented. Under legislation enacted there in 1983, every large coal-fired plant in West Germany which will operate past 1993 is being required to install and operate a high-efficiency FGD system by the beginning of 1988.

Cost information from West Germany shows capital cost of about $100 per kilowatt for a typical 350 megawatt retrofit, with lower cost for larger plants. Those figures are roughly half, or even less, than the estimates acid rain control opponents use to persuade the public that fixing the problem here would be too costly.

The issue of cost is an interesting one. The Reagan administration and the industries involved say it would be too expensive to scrub out the pollution before it contaminates the air. The West German experience shows they are wrong, and, moreover, the real cost equation should include the price of the damage caused by acid rain and the financial benefits we would gain from eliminating or reducing it.

A recent Regulatory Impact Analysis on sulfur pollution, prepared by the staff of the Environmental Protection Agency, examined the effects on health and welfare of several alternative pollution standards, including one standard that would reduce sulfur dioxide emissions by about 11 million tons per year—a reduction comparable to a number of acid rain control bills now pending in Congress. What is noteworthy about this study is that even though only a small fraction of potential benefits were quantified, very large economic benefits, in the neighborhood of $5 billion annually, would result.

Specifically, $2.4 billion of the benefits attributed by the EPA flow from reducing the economic costs associated with sulfate-related illness (lost wages and medical bills) and household soiling due to sulfate pollution. The study points out that this estimate may understate illness-related benefits by a factor of three, because no attempt was made to place a value on reduced pain and suffering.

These figures and history, taken from public Congressional testimony by NRDC attorneys David Hawkins and Richard Ayres, show some of the dimensions of the acid rain problem as it was understood before this book was published. Ayres, Hawkins, Deborah Sheiman, David Doniger and others at NRDC, along with the National Clean Air Coalition, are working daily to achieve the necessary legislative victory to reverse the conditions which Robert Mello has described here so poignantly.

NRDC is proud to join Island Press in publishing *Last Stand of the Red Spruce* in the hope that the author's next investigation can be focused on the story of how acid rain control measures began to bring the forests of America and Canada back to life.

Paul J. Allen
Director of Communications
Natural Resources Defense Council
July 1987

Acknowledgments

A great number of people helped make this book possible. As I reread the manuscript I realize how heavily I leaned on the published work of scores of scientists who have devoted large parts of their careers to the study of air pollution and forest decline. Their names are listed with the references in the bibliography and to each I owe a debt of thanks.

Several scientists agreed to review and comment on the manuscript at various stages of this project. Dr. Hubert W. Vogelmann, Dr. Richard M. Klein and Tim Scherbatskoy of the University of Vermont, Dr. Christina D. Runcie of Starksboro, Vermont, Dr. Kenneth D. Kimball of the Appalachian Mountain Club's Research Department in Pinkham Notch, New Hampshire, and Dr. David T. Funk of the Northeastern Forest Experiment Station, U.S.D.A. Forest Service in Durham, New Hampshire. Each spent several hours of time reviewing the manuscript and discussing it with me. Their criticisms and suggestions, particularly those of Dr. Vogelmann, were invaluable. To Dr. Thomas G. Siccama of the Yale School of Forestry and Environmental Studies, Dr. Robert I. Bruck of North Carolina State University, and Dr. Robert A. Gregory of the U.S.D.A. Forest Service in Burlington, Vermont, I also extend my thanks for discussing their work with me either in person or by telephone. Although this book would not exist without the help of these people, the content of these pages is my responsibility alone.

I am indebted to Honorable Jonathan B. Lash, Secretary of Vermont's Agency of Environmental Conservation, for his personal encouragement and suggestions of other people who might be helpful.

I also wish to thank Mr. Peter Borrelli, Editor of *The Amicus Journal*, for taking a special interest in the manuscript and for introducing me to Island Press. No first-time author ever received more professional, thoughtful or patient help from a publisher than I have received from the staff of Island Press, and especially from Ms. Barbara Dean, Executive Editor.

I am particularly grateful to Senator Patrick J. Leahy of Vermont for his gracious contribution and to the Natural Resources Defense Council for their cooperation with Island Press in the publication of this book.

Other who have helped in special ways include Mr. William Mares, Mr. Russell A. Reidinger, Ms. Joanne Aja Simpson, Ms. Martha Mutz, Ms. Mary R. Mello, Ms. Kim Frapier, and Mr. Robert and Ms. Gretchen Babcock.

To John H. Downs, Esquire, my friend and former law partner and Ms. Virginia Downs, friend and author, I am deeply grateful for their untiring support and encouragement and their painstaking review of the multiple revisions of the manuscript.

Finally, I owe the most to my friend and co-adventurer, Ms. Priscilla K. Reidinger, who debated every important point with me in a constructive manner and who never let me forget that my job was inquiry first and advocacy second.

Robert A. Mello
Hinesburg, Vermont
July, 1987

Atop Mt. Greylock, 1844

As the light in the east steadily increased, it revealed to me more clearly the new world into which I had risen in the night, the new terra-firma perchance of my future life. There was not a crevice left through which the trivial places we name Massachusetts, or Vermont, or New York, could be seen, while I still inhaled the clear atmosphere of a July morning—if it were July there. All around beneath me was spread for a hundred miles on every side, as far as the eye could reach, an undulating country of clouds, answering in the varied swell of its surface to the terrestrial world it veiled. It was such a country as we might see in dreams, with all the delights of paradise. There were immense snowy pastures, apparently smooth-shaven and firm, and shady vales between the vaporous maintains, and far in the horizon I could see where some luxurious misty timber jutted into the prairie, and trace the windings of a water course, some unimagined Amazon or Orinoko, by the misty trees on its brink. As there was wanting the symbol, so there was not the substance of impurity, no spot nor stain. . . .

Henry David Thoreau, 1844
atop Mt. Greylock in the
Berkshires

Thoreau in the Mountains: Writings by *Henry David Thoreau*. Commentary by William Howarth. Farrar Straus Giroux, N. Y. (1982), p. 76.

Introduction

The first mountain I climbed was Camels Hump (elev. 4,083') in the Green Mountains of northern Vermont. It was a small adventure, but unforgettable. The anticipation of discovery so heightened my senses that images, smells and sounds encountered on the way remain vivid in my mind today. That was almost fifteen years ago, yet I can still close my eyes and feel the sense of awe that washed over me then. I have climbed dozens of mountains throughout the United States since, most of them higher, some sporting finer views, and many hosting a greater variety of flora and fauna. Camels Hump remains my favorite.

Not everything in these mountains was beautiful, however. On numerous peaks throughout northern New York and New England I saw extraordinary numbers of dead and dying red spruce trees at high elevations. In some areas the sight was appalling. Dead trees were strewn in all directions, their fallen trunks and broken branches blocking the hiking trails. Before 1982, I knew nothing about the possible causes of this or about the commercial and ecological importance of the red spruce. Nevertheless, it always pained me to see such magnificent trees in distress, and the detrimental effect their destruction had on the magnificent forest landscape.

In the November 1982 issue of *Natural History*, I read an article entitled ''Catastrophe on Camels Hump'' written by Dr. Hubert W. Vogelmann, Chairman of the Department of Botany of the University of Vermont. I learned that scientists had been monitoring the condition of the red spruce on that peak since the mid-1960s, and that the condition of the trees was a major concern to the scientific community. Inventories of Camels Hump and other mountains in the Northeast showed that spruce-fir forests in the region had been in a significant and accelerating state of decline since the early 1960s. I also learned that the cause was both mysterious and controversial.

Some ecologists believed that a condition known as acid rain was killing forest trees here as well as in parts of Europe, and that the demise of the red spruce was the first stage of a potentially greater environmental disaster. Other scientists believed that natural causes alone could account for the condition of the forests and that the red spruce would return to full vigor in time. After reading the article, I promised myself that someday I would look more deeply into these conflicting arguments.

View of Camels Hump, Vermont from Satellite, 1987.
Source: U. S. Geological Survey.

I am a trial lawyer. In July 1984, I was a partner in Vermont's largest law firm when I began a one year sabbatical. This was my chance to find out why these magnificent trees were dying on my favorite mountain. I had no fixed views as to whether or not the acid rain theory was valid, or whether natural phenomena were the cause. My research was carried out independently of any interest groups. Nor did I seek any funding or help from the many environmental groups and industrial associations concerned with the problem of acid rain.

This book is the result of a year of almost full-time research into scientific endeavors to track down the true causes of the decline of our eastern forests, particularly the forests of the Adirondack, Green Mountain and White Mountain regions. My research included study of nearly 200 articles written by American, Canadian, European, and Scandinavian scientists that have been published in dozens of technical journals. I also interviewed some of the ecologists, botanists, plant pathologists and plant physiologists who have been in the forefront of research on this subject. These interviews in turn gave me access to much unpublished scientific material. In addition, I have hiked many of the affected mountains.

I found through my research that some of the most important discoveries about the effects of air pollution on our forests have not been disseminated outside the scientific literature, and thus are largely inaccessible to the public. I have attempted in my study to make important information about the public policy issues surrounding air pollution and forest health available and understandable to the general public. I am an amateur naturalist, and I make no claim to scientific expertise. I did however, ask a number of professional scientists with differing views on the theories of air pollution damage to forest trees to review and comment on the manuscript before publication. Their comments were immensely helpful. It would be impossible to review in one book the sum total of scientific knowledge about the effects of air pollution on forest trees. In the context of my own enquiry, it seemed appropriate to focus primarily on the efforts of four American scientists to discover why red spruce trees are dying in northern New York and New England. The red spruce is commercially more important than most other forest trees; it has been studied by scientists more closely than any other species in the United States, and it is the forest tree species most severely affected by acid rain. The decline of the red spruce over the last 30 years has been so severe that there is reason to fear it may disappear altogether. Two of the scientists whose work I have focused on believe that air pollution is killing the red spruce and other trees. The other two have been vocal critics of that view. This controversy gave me the opportunity to present both sides of an issue that has divided the American scientific community.

After months of reading the scientific literature, I felt a growing alarm. Whether or not the link between air pollution and our dying forests is—or ever will be—proven beyond a doubt, it seems to me that the most recent scientific discoveries compel us to reassess the need to control air pollution in this country. My second reason for writing this book, then is to urge that reassessment. Many theories have been offered and tested, but in my own view, none explains the decline of our forests as completely as the air pollution theory. I believe that the circumstantial evidence implicating air pollution is sufficiently impressive that legislative action should be taken immediately to reduce emissions substantially in the hope of protecting our forests from the risk of greater damage. We should also do what we can to ameliorate the considerable damage that has already been done. Yet action to accomplish these goals will take place only if the public is informed of the facts that indicate the need for such action.

The quality of our lives would be diminished without the forest products we rely on daily. Each year, tens of thousands set out to hike and camp in the beautiful forests of the northeastern United States. So our forest resources offer not only commerce and recreation, but also inspiration. A mountaineer never forgets the first climb or loses the urge to climb again. Our children and their children are entitled to the opportunity to stand in awe of the majesty of unspoiled nature and to contemplate its meaning. Only we can preserve it for them.

1

Death in the Boreal Zone

The red spruce (*Picea rubens* Sarg.) brings beauty and grace to the most inhospitable climatic zone our eastern mountains have to offer, the montane boreal zone. In northern New England and New York this subarctic band extends from approximately 3,000 feet above sea level to the tree line; in the southern Appalachians it begins at about 5,000 feet and encompasses all the highest peaks. In this zone of fierce winds and severe cold, the growing season is short, and the soils are thin, rocky, and infertile. Yet the red spruce survives, often growing in pure stands and can live to be nearly 400 years old. Few other trees survive in the boreal zone. In the northern Appalachians only red spruce, balsam fir, and white birch can cope with such climatic conditions. Without these species, the upper third of the mountains would be mostly bare, eroded rock. These were the trees Thoreau saw jutting through the clouds over Vermont.

In the autumn of 1982, Dr. Hubert W. Vogelmann, Chairman of the Department of Botany at the University of Vermont, reported that the red spruces were dying in the virgin forests on the slopes of Camels Hump, a high peak of the northern Green Mountains of Vermont. Since 1965, when the forests there were inventoried, nearly half of the red spruces had died, some of which had been seedlings when Samuel de Champlain discovered Vermont in 1609. These young red spruces and their towering companions had dominated the vast expanses of high elevation and later had inspired the early settlers to give Vermont and her Green Mountains their names. Vogelmann described what he saw in an article entitled ''Catastrophe on Camels Hump'' published by *Natural History* in November 1982:[1]

Gray skeletons of trees, their branches devoid of needles, are everywhere in the forest. Trees young and old are dead, and most of those still alive bear brown needles and have unhealthy looking crowns. . . . As more and more trees die and are blown down, the survivors have less protection from the wind, and even they are toppled over. The forest looks as if it has been struck by a hurricane.[2]

Ordinarily, red spruces reseed quickly and heavily. As the great evergreens died and opened the canopy of the treetops, the bare forest floors became bathed in life-giving sunshine. Although an explosion of shrubs and other new vegetation followed, Vogelmann reported that there are no young spruces to be seen.[3]

Vogelmann, a field botanist and ecologist for twenty years, has always preferred field work to library or laboratory study. His extensive investigations have earned him national recognition and awards from The Nature Conservancy, Syracuse University, the U.S. Environment Protection Agency, and others. Since earning his doctorate from the University of Michigan in 1955, Vogelmann has conducted several field studies in marshes, swamps, and high elevation cloud forests from Canada to South America. His first ecological investigations focused on the arctic and subarctic vegetation of the Knob Lake region of Quebec, Canada. In 1964, Vogelmann began a series of botanical explorations in the Andes Mountains, the Putumayo, and the upper Amazon basin of Colombia, South America. The following year the Botanical Museum of Harvard University sent him back to Colombia to collect specimens of medicinal plants. From 1966 to 1970, Vogelmann conducted another series of studies as a National Science Foundation Teaching Fellow in the tropical cloud forests on the Sierra Madre Oriental Mountains of eastern Mexico. The majority of Vogelmann's field work, however, has been in the high-elevation arctic and subarctic zones of the northern Appalachian Mountains; consequently, by 1979 he was very familiar with the red spruce.

The red spruce, one of North America's most beautiful, hardy and valuable trees, is a luxuriant evergreen with a thick, shiny coat of dark green needles. A dramatic conifer, it grows to be one hundred feet tall and stands in an open field like a pyramid, with regular whorls of branches rising along its straight mastlike trunk. The red spruce was named because of the cylindrical reddish-brown cones that hang from its branches.

The habitat of the red spruce is relatively small and in the U.S. is closely associated with the Appalachian Mountains, which offer the wet and cool climate that spruce trees like best. Its natural range extends from Nova Scotia and New Brunswick southwestward to North Carolina and Tennessee. The further south one goes to find red spruce, the higher up the mountains one must climb. In the northern extreme of its range, red spruce grow from near sea level up to an elevation of about 4,500 feet; in the Great Smoky Mountains at the southern end of its range, red spruces grow from elevations of about 4,500 to 6,500 feet. Of the eight spruce species that live in North America, only three (red spruce, white spruce, and black spruce) live in the East and, of these, the red spruce alone grows south of upper West Virginia.

Commercially, the red spruce was once one of the most valuable softwoods in America; today, it is still the most important of the spruces. Since red spruce at one time made up approximately 80 percent of the eastern spruce volume, the paper and construction industries have traditionally relied on it heavily for pulpwood and timber. The red spruce's long, straight trunk attains a diameter of three or four feet, making its logs a lumberman's prize. By the late 1930s, red spruces in both the northern and southern Appalachians had been so heavily and repeatedly logged that the tree had nearly disappeared from more than a million acres of forest land. Its exploitation prompted some ecologists even then to express concern about the tree's ability to recover its lost territory; forty years later, ecologists discovered a much more serious cause for concern.

In 1979, Vogelmann and his colleagues discovered that red spruces were dying inexplicably and prematurely. This evidence indicated that the decline of the trees was not only continuing, but accelerating. Three years later, when Vogelmann published his article in *Natural History*, the decline was still accelerating, and was not confined to Camels Hump. These trees were dying on the Appalachian Mountains from West Virginia to New England, on the Adirondack Mountains of New York, in the White Mountains of New Hampshire, in the Laurentian Mountains of Quebec, and throughout the Green Mountains of northern Vermont. Red spruces of various ages covering an enormous geographical area were dying simultaneously of unknown causes. Vogelmann observed that the greatest damage was occurring in the evergreen forests located at high elevations and on the slopes facing windward: "It is a disaster that, in a few short years, has dramatically changed the appearance of high mountains."[4]

As a result of this sudden decline of the red spruce, scientists in the Northeast began trying to discover as quickly as possible the identity of the destructive forces at work. Forest environments are complex and require time to understand, but time was not on their side. Some prominent scientists viewed the dead evergreens as the omen of an impending environmental disaster, one that could eliminate the red spruce and possibly spread to other forest species. Yet, without a sound diagnosis, no reliable treatment could be offered to the remaining, embattled spruces.

(Above) Tree bark affected by fungus.
(Left) Forester points out galleries in a spruce bark infested by the eastern spruce bark beetle. Source: USDA Forest Service.

2

Three Great Natural Enemies

The forest has three great natural enemies—fire, insects, and fungi. In North America, more mature timber has been destroyed by this formidable triumvirate than has been harvested by man. Since no fires of any known consequence had occurred on Camels Hump since 1965, the first of the three could be ruled out. This still left a variety of diseases and pests as potential villains. If a recognized insect or fungus could be found attacking the dead and dying red spruce trees, then the cause of the decline would be known quickly and with certainty. Therefore, Vogelmann and the others began their investigations here.

Although many insects are known to attack red spruce, only three are voracious enough to kill the trees in large numbers. The spruce budworm, considered one of the most dangerous of all the forest insects, has devastated more spruces and balsams in the Northeast than any other. Several serious outbreaks of budworm in Canada and New England killed a considerable part of the affected forests. The most catastrophic outbreak on record began in northern Quebec about 1909 and spread southward into New England. By the time the epidemic was over in 1923, more than 200,000,000 cords of balsam fir and many millions of cords of spruce timber had been destroyed. The budworm, a defoliator, eats the buds and new needles of the red spruces in the spring, causing the trees to weaken and often to die. Trees, weakened by the loss of foliage, then become targets of another enemy—the eastern spruce bark beetle—which burrows under the bark of the tree. The tree promptly dies from the attack of the beetles and by the penetration of lethal fungi through the openings made by insects.

The European spruce sawfly is another defoliator; it eats the old needles of the red spruce until the current year's new needles mature; then it eats them too. The sawfly has also caused an enormous loss of mature red spruce timber in the northeastern United States. The last outbreak of spruce sawfly in Vermont occurred in the late 1930s, leaving several thousands of acres of spruce forests in central and southern Vermont severely infested. Defoliated spruces were also found on Mt. Ellen, Mt. Abraham, and Mt. Battell near Lincoln, and on Green Peak in Dorset, Vermont.

Modern silvicultural management techniques combined with chemical spraying have helped control insect populations in recent years. The war against the spruce budworm and other enemies of the red spruce, however, was not yet won. In 1982 spruce-fir forests in Canada and Maine were blighted by another devastating epidemic of spruce budworm. More than 5 million acres of evergreen forests were infested in Maine, the nation's leading producer of paper products. Therefore, when Vogelmann searched Camels Hump for prime suspects to blame for the dying red spruces, he naturally put insects high on the list. This suspect had to be taken off the list, however, when the scientist reported that "we have not found any insects on Camels Hump that could cause the current mortality."[1]

With insects ruled out as the cause of decline, scientists turned their attention to germs. The task of identifying a treekilling disease belongs to the plant pathologist. For the pathologist, the innumerable chemical, microscopic, physical, climatic and environmental components that can be gathered, examined, measured, tested, and analyzed from the ground up provide only half of the story. The other half remains underground.

The roots of many trees are measured in miles. For some, the area of the roots may exceed the area of the tree that towers above. The chemistry of the ground where the roots must live is more diverse and complex than the chemistry of air, and there is a greater variety of visible and invisible life in the ground than above it. There are more than one hundred thousand species of fungi alone; pick up a gram of dry soil and you will be holding in your hand up to one million fungal spores. That does not even count the myriad bacteria, viruses, and mycoplasma that are borne by the soil. This subterranean world of trees is, therefore, of great concern to the pathologist.

Fungi are the most common, significant cause of tree diseases. Nearly two thousand species of fungi have been found to infect trees. The most serious fungal infections are those that attack and rot the roots of forest trees and other plants.* The red spruce, however, suffers from few serious diseases. The tree is naturally resistant to many common pathogens. If a red spruce is injured or stressed by an external cause, it may then be susceptible to invasion by a host of deadly soilborne and airborne fungi that cause severe rotting of its roots and heartwood, cankers, defoliation, rusts, and death. But as long as the red spruce is healthy and exhibiting good growth, it has the inherent ability to resist the entrance or subsequent development of fungi even when environmental conditions are suitable for their growth.

Dr. Philip M. Wargo, a plant pathologist with the U.S. Forest Service, along with several scientists from the Yale School of Forestry and Environmental Studies, extensively surveyed red spruces on Camels Hump and eight other mountains in Vermont, New Hampshire, Massachusetts, and New York to see whether

---

*It was a fungus, *Phytophthora infestans*, that rotted up to one half of potato crops from Ireland to Russia from 1845 to 1860, resulting in starvation for millions of people and the mass immigration of millions more to the United States.

a disease organism was responsible for the mortality. They examined 288 healthy, sick, dead, and dying red spruce trees. They found a fungus, *Armillaria mellea*, on the roots of dead and declining red spruces at all elevations. The more advanced the infection, the sicker the tree.

Responsible for one of the most severe tree root diseases of all the fungi, *Armillaria mellea* is native to most forest soils worldwide, including the northeastern United States. It attacks and kills the roots of many kinds of hardwood and softwood trees. Trees infected by it usually die. At first, the needles of a victim may turn a pale, yellowish-green and fall prematurely or remain undersized or scanty. As the tree's overall growth rate slows down, the growth and foliage at the crown begin to deteriorate. In the advanced stages, as its needles turn brown and fall, the tree looks like it is dying from the top down and from the outside in. As the disease progressively kills and rots away the roots, the tree loses its support and becomes easily broken or uprooted by the wind. When the tree is dead or nearly so, honey-colored toadstools may appear at the base of the tree, producing billions of spores that will be carried by the winds to infect other susceptible trees in the forest.

These were the very symptoms that Vogelmann saw on the dead and dying red spruces on Camels Hump and elsewhere. Nevertheless, the pathologists determined that *Armillaria mellea* was not the cause of the disaster. Like nearly all fungi it is a passive opportunist, almost never attacking or seriously harming a healthy tree. *Armillaria mellea* becomes dangerous to a red spruce only when some other primary force, such as unfavorable environmental conditions, poor soil, moisture imbalance, or insect defoliation weakens the tree and predisposes it to infection. Furthermore, the pathologists observed that the number of trees infected by *Armillaria mellea* was least in the very regions where the most trees were dead and dying. The intensity of the red spruce decline got worse the higher up the mountains the scientists ascended, and it was most prominent above elevations of 3,000 feet, where red spruce was most dominant; the opposite was true of the fungus. Above 3,000 feet 61 percent of the recently dead red spruces had no infection at all, and 91 percent of the severely declining trees were also free of infection. More red spruces were dying there in the absence of *Armillaria mellea* than in its presence.

In a research paper published in the *Plant Disease Journal*, the pathologists concluded that *Armillaria mellea*, the only disease organism found on the red spruces, was not the primary cause of the red spruce mortality:

The association of *A. mellea* with declining trees indicated that the trees are being predisposed to damage by some undetermined biotic or abiotic stress. The fact that trees are dying in the absence of *A. mellea* indicates that the stress is sufficient by itself to cause mortality or that other secondary organisms are interacting with the stress to kill the trees.[2]

Detailed scientific investigations conducted by knowledgeable specialists had ruled out the forest's three great natural enemies—fire, insects, and fungi—as primary causes of the red spruce decline. When events cannot be explained with certainty by the application of known scientific facts, the scientist must turn to the uncertain world of theory.

Thus Vogelmann, Dr. Richard M. Klein of the University of Vermont, and concerned scientists from Europe, Canada, and the

United States set out to identify the forces responsible for the widespread decline of these great trees. Their work would produce a thicket of related but opposing theories and hundreds of scientific reports published in dozens of journals in Europe and the United States. The competing theories they developed would divide the community of American botanists into several vocal factions, sometimes sending long-term colleagues on separate paths. In the process, Camels Hump came to be one of the most closely studied mountains in the world.

3

A Close Correlation

The signs of the red spruce decline were first discovered in Vermont in the early 1950s, but their significance was overlooked. For several years Dr. Paul V. Mook, the pathologist for the Northeastern Forest Experiment Station of the National Forest Service, had been receiving reports that mature red spruce trees were dying at high elevations in the Green Mountains. Entomologists who worked with Mook had ruled out insects as the cause. Therefore, in the spring of 1955 Mook and his biology aide, Harold G. Eno, joined officials of the Green Mountain National Forest to study the problem. Mook's primary purpose was to determine whether the mortality was attributable to fungal disease.

Mook and Eno studied 132 red spruce trees, 21 percent of which were dead. The trees they studied ranged from 140 to 369 years of age—their average age was 259 years. They were located above the 2,500-foot elevation on sites exposed to the elements. Mook found that only 6.4 percent of the volume of the trees was rotted, a surprisingly low figure considering the age of the trees. The two scientists wrote up their findings in a brief Research Note and then closed the case:

No positive evidence was obtained that the presence of rot affected the trees adversely other than to make them more liable to windfall. Experiment station entomologists had already eliminated insects as primary agents causing mortality, and this study also eliminated fungi. It therefore seems plausible to ascribe it to overmaturity of trees growing under severe environmental conditions on shallow and well—drained soils at high altitude. This theory is strengthened by general observations that the higher the elevation, the thinner and dryer the soils; and the steeper the slopes, the greater the losses.[1]

There was no discussion in the Research Note about how trees that can live to be over 300 would be dying of overmaturity at age 140. There was also no discussion of whether the trees might have been dying from air pollution. In 1955, scientists in the United States had not yet begun to believe that air pollution could harm a remote forest.

Inside the narrow band that extends from the ground to just 25 feet above the ground, 5 billion tons of air pass over the United States each day. For hundred of millions of years, this air has brought to trees the carbon dioxide, hydrogen, and water they need to live. Since the beginning of the Industrial Revolution, the air has also brought increasing amounts of noxious pollutants. The burning of oil and coal by electrical power plants and manufacturing facilities, the combustion of gasoline by motor vehicles, incineration, the smelting and refining of copper, lead, zinc, nickel, and other ores cumulatively pour tens of millions of tons of particles and gases into the atmosphere every year. All of the particles and gases that go up ultimately come back down either as fallout or in precipitation. While they are in the air, however, the pollutants undergo a chain of chemical reactions, transforming some of the gases into more dangerous forms of pollution; thus, what comes back out of the air is worse than what was put into it. Many of these pollutants are known to be deadly to trees, depending upon the concentrations present and the length of time the trees are exposed.

When sulfur and nitrogen combine with the most abundant, lifegiving element on earth, oxygen, they produce poisonous air pollutants. Free oxygen, which makes up about 21 percent of the volume of the air at the earth's surface, is an extremely active element; it can react and combine with nearly all of the other chemical elements. Sulfur is a pale-yellow chemical used to vulcanize rubber and to make gunpowder, insecticides, paper, and other products; it burns with a stifling odor. When sulfur bearing resources like coal and oil are burned, the hot sulfur combines with oxygen and is released into the atmosphere as sulfur dioxide (SO_2). The most important and widespread sulfur pollutant, sulfur dioxide, is a heavy, colorless, suffocating gas that is easily liquified. It is used as a bleach, a disinfectant, and in preservatives, among other things. Whenever green trees are subjected to high concentrations of sulfur dioxide in the air, their growth rates are reduced and they often die. Since a conifer's needles exchange carbon dioxide, oxygen, water vapor, and other gases with the air, there are many microscopic pores into which the sulfur dioxide gas can pass; when it does, the needles die, turn brown, and fall.

Nitrogen is a colorless, tasteless, odorless gas that makes up about 78 percent of the volume of the air at the earth's surface. Although nitrogen and oxygen coexist in the atmosphere, they do not combine, since these gases do not react together under natural conditions. When nitrogen-bearing resources like oil and coal are burned, however, the intense heat causes these building blocks of life to combine and form nitric oxide (NO), a colorless gaseous pollutant. In addition, the burning of gasoline, diesel fuel, and natural gas generates enough heat to cause the nitrogen and oxygen in the surrounding air to unite and form nitric oxide. Ever-present ultraviolet light from the sun then causes some of the nitric oxide to react again with oxygen and hydrocarbons to form nitrogen dioxide (NO_2), a poisonous reddish-brown gas. Nitric oxide and nitrogen dioxide are both toxic to trees in large concentrations, and the damage they inflict is similar to that caused by sulfur dioxide.

Fig. 1 — Transported Air Pollutants: Emissions to Effects.

As sulfur dioxide, nitrogen oxides, and hydrocarbons are carried away from their sources, they form a complex ''pollutant mix'' leading to acid deposition, ozone, and airborne fine particles. These transported air pollutants pose risks to surface waters, forests, crops, materials, visibility, and human health. Source: Office of Technology Assessment, *Acid Rain and Transported Air Pollutants*, 1984.

The chain reaction that progressively degrades the air does not end there. Some of the dangerous dioxides spawned by sulfur and nitrogen pollution, in turn, convert vital oxygen and water vapor into even more potent pollutants: ozone and acids. The same ultraviolet light that created nitrogen dioxide causes it to react with more oxygen to form ozone (O_3), an unstable pale-blue gas used by industry as a bleaching agent. Ozone is a prime part of urban smog. The damage it causes to evergreen foliage is similar to that of sulfur dioxide, nitric oxide and nitrogen dioxide, although ozone requires less time and smaller concentrations to achieve it. Strong mineral acids are also created in polluted air; however, their destructive pattern is both different and more severe.

When sulfur dioxide, nitric oxide, and nitrogen dioxide molecules mix in the atmosphere with water vapor and radical forms of water, many of them are oxidized, and hydrolyzed into sulfuric acid (H_2SO_4) and nitric acid (HNO_3). The chemical reactions that produce these highly corrosive, colorless acids can occur not only in the atmosphere but also in the soils and on surfaces, such as the leaves and needles of trees, wherever sulfur dioxide, nitric oxide, and nitrogen dioxide end up. The exact percentage of the gases that eventually returns to the earth in rain, fog, snow, fallout, etc., is unknown, but it is enough to erode marble statues, discolor paint, corrode metal, and destroy fish populations in remote rivers and lakes. (See Figure 1.) On the needles of evergreen trees like the red spruce, these acids can eat away at the waxy coatings that protect the needles from drying out, and can strip away the proteins, sugars and amino acids the needles need to live.

The term acid rain was coined in 1872 by an English chemist, Dr. Robert Angus Smith. For twenty years Smith studied the chemistry of the air and the rain in England, Scotland, and Germany. He discovered that the air in the city of Manchester, England,

and elsewhere contained particles of copper and other contaminants, and that it also contained sulfuric acid, which was corroding metal, fading clothing, and damaging plants. Smith also found that the chemistry of the precipitation in various areas depended upon such things as the amount of coal being burned and the direction the wind was blowing. His remarkable book, *Air and Rain: The Beginnings of a Chemical Climatology*, however, was approximately one hundred years ahead of its time. Smith's work was almost totally ignored by his colleagues and overlooked by subsequent generations.

The second scientist to make a major contribution to our knowledge about the causes and effects of air pollution, Dr. Eville Gorham, was also disregarded by his colleagues. Gorham, an English ecologist, studied how changes in the chemistry of precipitation affected the chemistry of surface waters and soils near industrialized centers in England and Canada. His research established that precipitation near industrial areas was acidic, that its acidity was caused by the emission of sulfur dioxide from the burning of fossil fuels, that acid rain and snow were increasing the acidity of lake waters, that acid precipitation was also acidifying soils and changing their chemistry, and that airborne sulfur dioxide and sulfuric acid were harming plants. Although he published his findings in many different scientific journals from 1955 to 1965, no one took him seriously or followed up on his work. It was not until the late 1960s that scientists in Europe began to see a connection between the air pollution originating in urban areas and the decline of great forest trees hundreds of miles away. In the United States this awareness did not come about until the early 1970s.

Populated areas in northern New York and New England produce little air pollution, because there are few large cities or industrial centers in the region. Because of the prevailing winds and storm stacks that sweep across the continental United States and Canada, air pollution is collected from distant regions and funnelled into the Northeast. Sulfur dioxide and other gases and particles emitted from the stacks of fossil fuel-burning plants in the Midwest, the South, and the Southeast generally remain in the air for several days, carried on wind currents for hundreds of miles until they either fall out of the atmosphere or are flushed out by precipitation. Since at least 1900, sulfur dioxide emissions in Ohio, Illinois, and other Midwestern states have been generally higher than in any other region of the United States, and nitric oxide emissions from those states have also been among the highest in the nation. (See Figure 2.) Also, the Southern and Southeastern parts of the U.S. have seen dramatic growth in industry and air pollution emissions since the 1950s. Tracks of frontal storms over the past century show where the pollution travels. (See Figure 3.) Five of the nation's six main storm tracks flow through the heavily industrialized Midwest and South; from there they either travel directly to the Northeast, or they are intercepted by other prevailing winds that do.

The geography and climate of the northern Appalachians furnish a number of features that efficiently filter pollution out of the passing air. There are frequent episodes of air inversion and air stagnation in the Northeast which give air pollutants an opportunity to accumulate and reach high concentrations. The Appalachian Range itself confronts the oncoming air masses with a series of high walls that force the air upward, where it cools and forms precipitation. As a result, the northeastern mountainous regions receive a great deal more precipitation than most other regions—50 to 70 inches per year at the higher elevations. The rain, fog, sleet, and snow effectively wash pollution out of the air

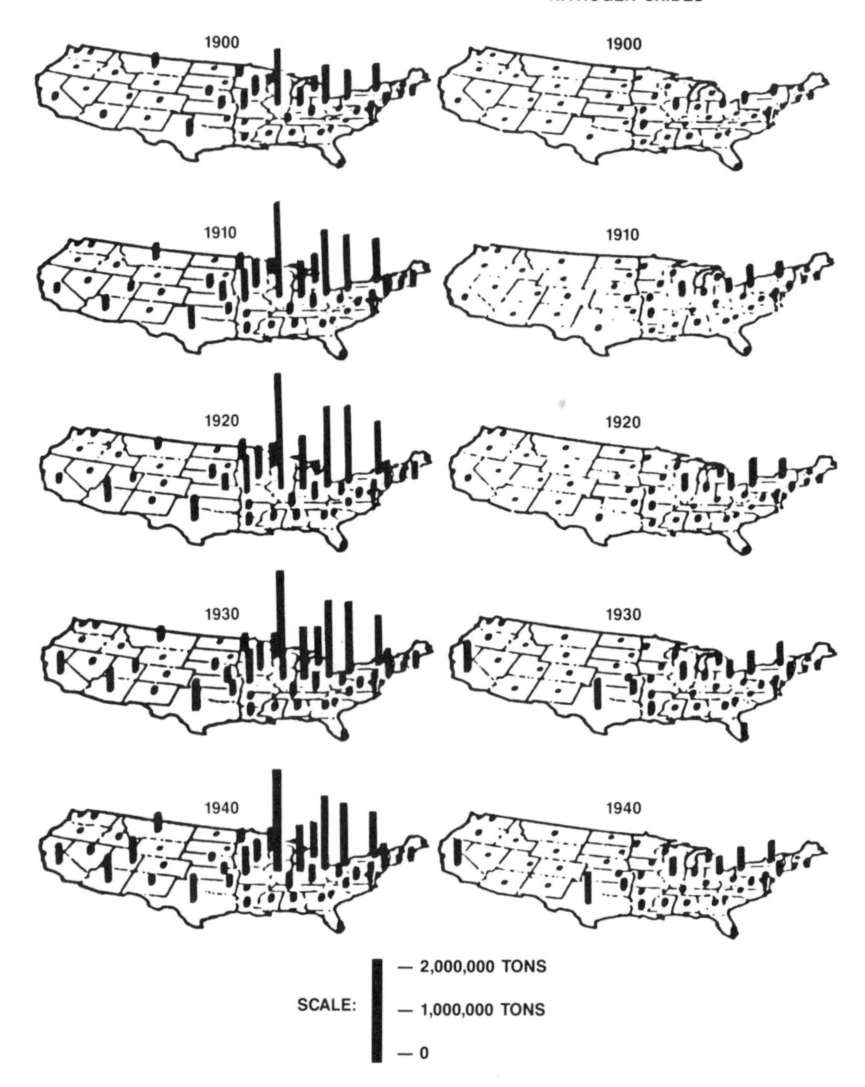

Fig. 2 — Emissions of SO_2 and NO_2 for Every Tenth Year, 1900-1980.

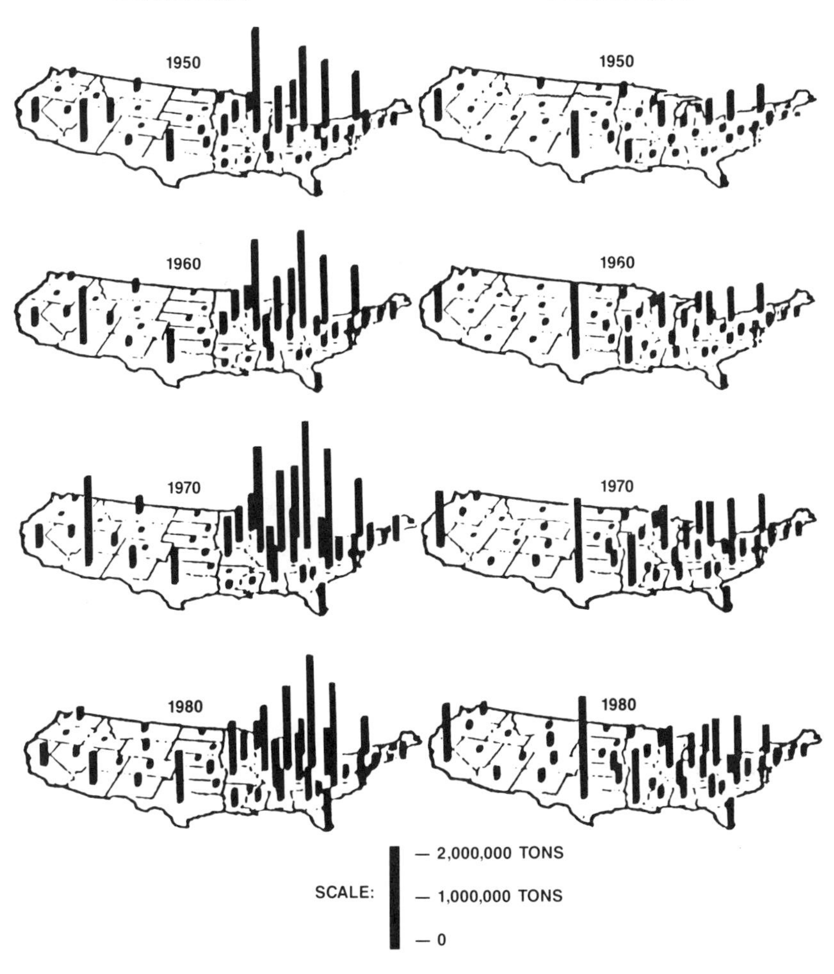

Source: Gschwandter, G., K. Gschwandter, K. Eldridge, C. Mann, and D. Mobley. Historic Emissions of Sulfur and Nitrogen Oxides in the United States from 1900 to 1980. *Journal of the Air Pollution Control Association*. Vol. 36, No. 2 (1986).

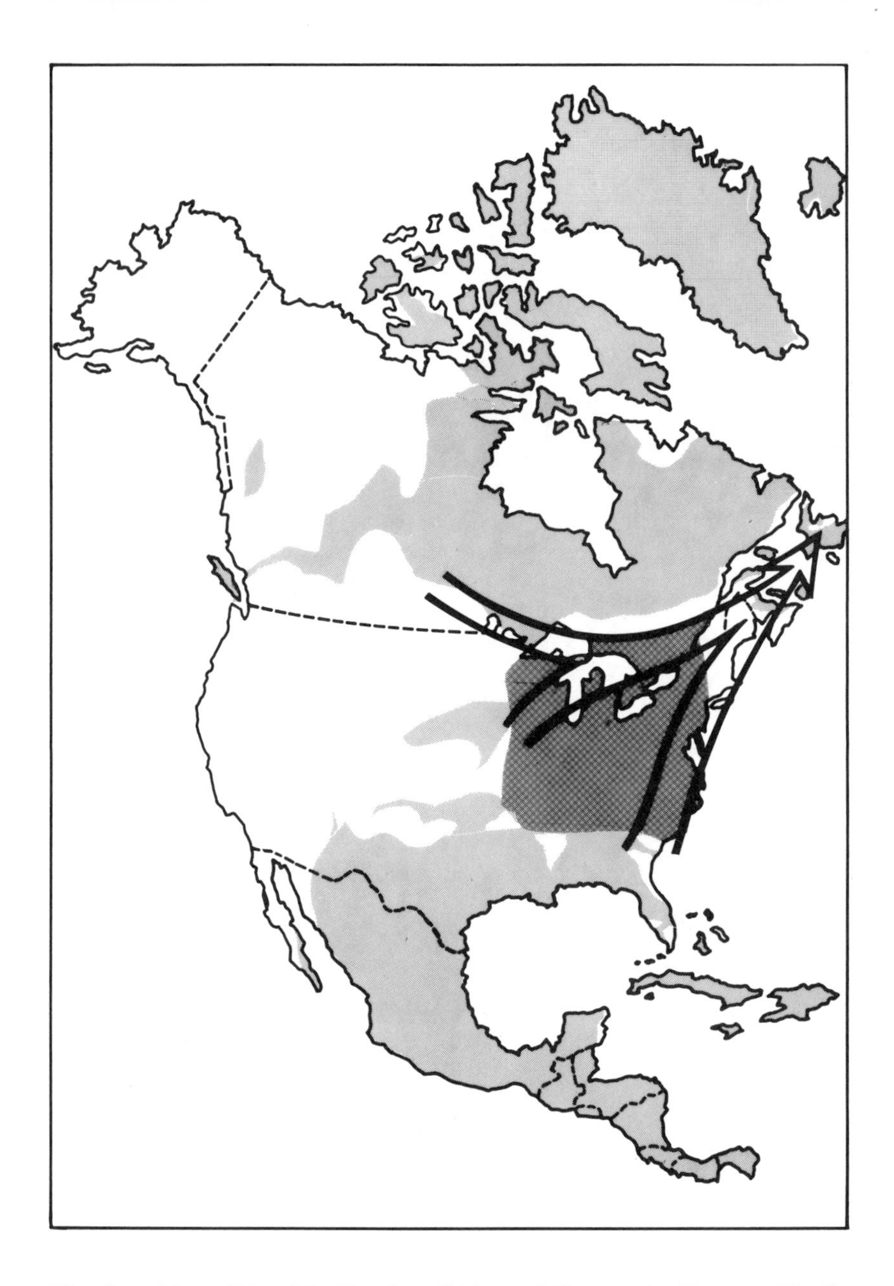

Fig. 3 — Mean Monthly Tracks of Frontal Storms in Eastern North America, 1885-1980.

Sixty-five percent of all sulfur dioxide and forty-nine percent of all nitrogen oxides produced in North America are emitted in the dark area to the west of New England. Source: F.H. Bormann, The Northeast Landscape: Air Pollution Stress and Energy Policy, *Ambio,* Vol. II, 1982, p. 192.

and into the soils below. Finally, the windy summits of the high Appalachians are crowned with rich evergreen forests that can remove chemicals from the air even when there is no stagnation or precipitation. As the prevailing westerly and southwesterly winds force the heavily polluted air mass over the mountains, the trees intercept the air and comb out the contaminants with their outstretched needles and branches.

In 1974, two ecologists, Dr. Gene E. Likens of Cornell University (later head of the prestigious Cary Arboretum of New York Botanical Garden) and Dr. F. Herbert Bormann of Yale University, became the first scientists in the United States to complete a comprehensive study of the chemistry of precipitation in the Northeast and to document the relationship between air pollution and the decline of great forest trees. Their discoveries arose out of a decade of intensive field and laboratory work at the Hubbard Brook Experimental Forest in the White Mountains of New Hampshire. Hubbard Brook included six watershed ecosystems maintained by the National Forest Service. Likens and Bormann had intended to study energy and nutrient cycles in cut and uncut forest ecosystems; in the process, they discovered surprising levels of acid rain and snow.

Likens and Bormann began monitoring the acidity of precipitation at Hubbard Brook in 1964, and they found it to be unnaturally acidic. Normal rainwater is slightly acidic, because water naturally reacts with carbon dioxide in the atmosphere and forms carbonic acid, a weak acid. By analyzing layers of frozen rainwater that had accumulated for centuries on glaciers throughout North America, scientists have determined that the acidity of natural rainwater is approximately 5.3 on the pH scale.*

---

*The pH scale was developed in 1909 by a Danish scientist named Sørensen to measure the degree of acidity of a solution. The symbol

From 1965 to 1971 the annual weighted average pH of the rain and snow that fell at Hubbard Brook ranged between 4.03 and 4.19; the lowest pH value recorded there during that period was an especially acidic 3.0, the acidity of white vinegar. Thus, the rain and snow that Likens and Bormann collected at Hubbard Brook was consistently and substantially more acidic than natural rainwater: the pH value of 3.0 measured at Hubbard Brook was several hundred times more acidic than normal precipitation. To Likens and Bormann this meant that weak carbonic acid had been replaced by strong mineral acids from the air as the predominant chemical components in precipitation. Their laboratory tests confirmed this; they found that 80 to 85 percent of the negatively charged ions in the precipitation came from sulfuric and nitric acids.

Likens and Bormann spoke to scientists in other states, reviewed the few studies reported in the scientific literature, and promoted tests in other locations to determine how widespread this acidity might be. They discovered that the problem was not limited to Hubbard Brook. Reports came in of pH readings made in 1970 and 1971 from a broad region: New Durham, New Hampshire: pH 4.27; Ithaca, Aurora, and Geneva in the Finger Lakes Region of upper New York: pH 3.91 to 4.02; Hubbardston, Massachusetts: pH 4.29; Thomaston, New Haven, and Killingsworth, Connecticut: 3.81 to 4.31. Similar reports came in from Maine, Vermont, and Rhode Island. The most shocking report came from the National Center for Atmospheric Research, which in November of

''pH'', which comes from a German term meaning ''hydrogen power'', is used to describe the concentration of electrically charged hydrogen atoms in a water solution. A pH of 7.0 means that the solution is neutral. Water becomes increasingly acidic at pH values below 7.0, and increasingly alkaline at values above 7.0. There is a tenfold difference between each unit of measure; thus, pH 6.0 is ten times more acidic than pH 7.0, and pH 5.0 is 100 times more acidic than pH 7.0, etc.

1964 had measured the precipitation of a storm in the Northeast at pH 2.1, the acidity of lemon juice.

Regions of the nation such as California, Oregon, and Florida, which were not located downwind from large industrial centers, did not share the problem; the pH of their precipitation was generally normal. The distribution pattern of other industrial pollutants such as lead was similar to the pattern of precipitation pH. Lead deposited annually from precipitation and fallout increased across the United States from 10 to 20 grams per hectare in the West and Midwest to over 1,000 near East Coast cities. In articles published in *Environment* and in *Science*, Likens and Bormann concluded: "it is apparent that the precipitation falling on most of the northeastern U.S. is characterized by high acidity"[2] and "that precipitation falling in northeastern United States is significantly more acidic than elsewhere in the United States."[3]

Since no one in the past had kept a long-term record of precipitation acidity, Likens and Bormann painstakingly searched through government and university libraries and unpublished records to piece together the evidence needed to establish the point in history when acidity changed from the norm of pH 5.3 to the extraordinary range of pH 3.8 to 4.3 in the Northeast. They found that the change in acidity occurred shortly after 1950, which was exactly when Mook and Eno discovered red spruce trees dying in large numbers on the Green Mountains of Vermont.

Before the early 1930s, coal and wood were the principal fuels used by homes, businesses, and industries in the United States. Coal contains not only large amounts of sulfur, but also large particles of calcium and other alkaline chemicals capable of neutralizing acids. As the coal burned, these particles of ash in the smoke reacted with the sulfur and sulfur dioxide, neutralizing the sulfuric acid as it was formed in the air. As a result, large particles of bothersome, but relatively harmless, soot constantly fell from the air locally in the vicinity of the chimneys and smokestacks. In response to increasing local complaints about soot, more and more industries over the years installed taller and taller stacks, fitting them with precipitators designed to remove the larger soot particles from the smoke. With the alkaline particles gone from the smoke, increasing quantities of intact sulfur dioxide gas spewed out of stacks hundreds of feet tall. From there the gas could be carried by winds to places far removed from the local vicinity.

In the early part of this century, most sulfur dioxide gas was emitted from stacks less than 240 feet tall. Since 1945, however, the reverse has been true. In 1950 only five percent of the sulfur dioxide gas pollution in the United States came from stacks taller than 480 feet. By 1980, however, stacks as tall and taller accounted for approximately 30 percent of all sulfur dioxide emissions nationally. Thus, by the early 1950s these changes had converted local soot problems into a growing regional acid phenomenon.

Other major events such as the Great Depression of the early 1930s, the World War II industrial effort in the early 1940s, and the coal miners' strike of 1945 affected the price and availability of coal and its major competitors, oil and natural gas. As more and more industries and homes converted from coal to oil, the shift in the predominant form of sulfur in the air intensified. Oil, like coal, contains large amounts of sulfur, but it does not contain the neutralizing alkaline substances. Therefore, the widespread conversion from coal and wood to oil further added to the volume of unneutralized sulfur dioxide in the atmosphere. At the same time, natural gas was gaining as a major source of fuel in the United States. Before 1950, natural gas constituted only 20 to 30 percent of the fuel used for commercial, industrial and residential purposes in the Ithaca and Geneva, New York, areas; by the early 1950s, however, 70 percent of the fuel used there was natural gas.

This regional trend in the consumption of natural gas mirrored a nationwide increase in usage; from 1950 to 1980, the total consumption of natural gas in the United States more than doubled. Since the burning of natural gas causes nitric oxide to form in the air, this change in the trends of fuel consumption and preference contributed further to the acid problem.

In 1950, the total level of sulfur dioxide gas emitted into the atmosphere in the United States was approximately the same as it had been in 1930. Between 1950 and 1970, however, the amount of sulfur dioxide gas poured into the air nationally increased by 45 percent to approximately 32 million tons annually. The trend in nitric oxide gas emissions was even more dramatic. From 1930 to 1950, total national nitric oxide gas emissions increased 20 percent to approximately 10 million tons. By 1970, however, the emission levels of this pollutant had risen another 90 percent to 19 million tons per year. (See Figure 2.)

Likens and Bormann found that before the early 1950s, the pH values of precipitation in the Northeast had been consistently normal—after that the readings were consistently and strongly acidic. Likens continued to monitor the changes in the acidity of precipitation in the United States for several years. He found that the intensity of the acidity worsened and that the areas covered expanded uninterruptedly over time.

In 1981, Likens published three maps of the United States in an article he coauthored with his technician, Mr. Thomas J. Butler, a colleague from Cornell. The maps, which appeared in *Atmospheric Environment*, looked like topographs with contour lines to show elevations, except that the lines on these maps depicted the increasing territory and intensity of acid precipitation. Each map charted the acidity scene at a different period of time to show long-term trends in precipitation. From 1955 to 1956, New York,

Vermont, and New Hampshire experienced rain and snow with pH values of less than 4.6. Ten years later, from 1965 to 1966, the precipitation in parts of New York, Vermont, and New Hampshire had become severely acidic, with a pH value of 4.3. By 1975 to 1976 the area covered with precipitation of pH 4.3 had spread to include an extensive region, and parts of New York and Vermont were regularly receiving rain and snow with a pH close to 4.0. Each of the circles grew larger over time and covered expanded regions with increasingly acidic precipitation. From 1955 to 1956 the territory receiving precipitation with a pH of less than 5.3 stretched southward to include parts of South Carolina and Georgia, and westward to include parts of Tennessee, Kentucky, Indiana, and Michigan. By 1975 to 1976 the acid rain territory had grown to include nearly all of Florida, Georgia, and Alabama and large parts of Mississippi, Arkansas, Missouri, and Illinois. By then even distant cities in the West located downwind from Seattle, Washington, and San Francisco and Los Angeles, California, were beginning to report pH values for precipitation substantially below 5.3: Berkeley, Pasadena, and Lake Tahoe, California, pH 4.06 to 5.0; the North Cascade Range of Washington, pH 4.85; Boulder, Colorado, pH 4.63.

As the evidence of acidity first started coming in during those early years at Hubbard Brook, Likens and Bormann became concerned about the effect that the pollution could be having on the forests there. They had good reasons to be concerned. Many of the gases and particles in the polluted air passing overhead were known to be toxic to trees; when present in high concentrations, they could inflict severe injury in a short time. Many scientists feared that the pollutants could also cause serious harm even at low concentrations if trees were exposed to them for long periods, but no one in the United States had yet documented a relationship between air pollution and the decline of any remote forest. In 1974, after ten years of work, Likens and Bormann became the first to do so.

The acidity of rain was a special concern to Likens and Bormann for two reasons. First, the precipitation in the Northeast was generally most acidic during the growing season. The higher relative humidity of the air during the summer accelerates the process of converting oxides into acids. Also, the acidity of the precipitation was changing the acidity of the forest soils throughout the region. Forty inches of rain at a pH of 4.0 will dump onto every acre of forest land almost a pound of the electrically charged hydrogen atoms that make acids caustic. There are millions of acres of forest land in the northern Appalachians, and the highest elevations regularly receive substantially more precipitation than forty inches. As a result, in the Adirondacks, the Green Mountains, and the White Mountains, the soils below the 2,500-foot elevation had a pH of 4.5 to 5.5, and the soils above 2,500 feet where the red spruces live had pH values ranging from 3.0 in the early spring to 4.5 in the late summer. The pH range within which red spruce thrives was generally believed to be 4.0 to 5.5. And some scientists were questioning whether it could thrive at pH value approaching 4.0; they had found that spruce and fir trees grown under certain conditions began to show damage at pH values of 4.1 to 4.4.

There were a number of other warning signs that collectively indicated special danger for the high-elevation conifers like the red spruce. Evergreens were known to be more sensitive to injury by sulfur dioxide and other gaseous pollutants than deciduous trees, partly because the needles of the evergreens remained exposed all year. Broadleaf trees like maples were able to withstand higher concentrations of sulfur dioxide in the air, in part because they enjoyed a respite each autumn and winter. Moreover, the high-elevation spruce-fir forests were exposed to two kinds of especially severe acidic precipitation—clouds and fogs—that lower elevations ordinarily did not experience.

When Henry David Thoreau scanned Vermont from the top of Mt. Greylock, the air was still clean. By 1974, however, the clouds and fogs that enveloped the mountaintops of the northern Green Mountains for up to 2,000 hours per year had become full of poisonous chemicals. Cloud and fog moisture, averaging pH 3.7 during the growing season, is consistently more acidic than acid rain or snow, and it contains higher concentrations of cadmium, copper, zinc, and lead. The turbulent eddies of air and greater wind speeds found at high elevations cause this polluted moisture to be intercepted by the evergreen foliage. Scientists, walking through these forests in the summer, frequently find them dripping with water even when it has not rained. In the winter, passing clouds cover the needles and branches of the spruces and firs with a frozen coat of hoarfrost several inches thick. Based upon years of field work in the White Mountains, Dr. William A. Reiners and others from Dartmouth College have estimated that this process of cloud and fog interception adds to the subalpine canopy another three inches of precipitation for every four inches that fall on it as rain and snow each year. Researchers have found the same to be true on the highest peaks of the Green Mountains of Vermont.

Hubbard Brook furnished a good location for assessing whether the growth rate of a remote forest was affected by chronic exposures to air pollution originating hundreds of miles away. Since it was located between the 1,800- and 2,600-foot elevation, Hubbard Brook included portions of both the hardwood forest (dominated by sugar maple, yellow birch, and American beech) and the transitional forest (inhabited by mountain maple and red spruce), which leads to the boreal zone above. In addition, it was a relatively young and even-aged forest. Historical records established that the entire watershed had been logged shortly after the turn of the century. Spruces were cut first around 1909, and the rest of the merchantable timber was cleared about 1917. The trees still standing at Hubbard Brook fifty years later had been too young and small for the loggers to harvest. Since the forest was a young one, it would naturally be expected to show strong and steady growth for the entire study period, and long after. Any interruption in its growth rate up through the 1960s, therefore, would be detectable, abnormal, and telling.

Unless trees are actually dying in large numbers, one cannot tell how well they are growing in a forest just by looking at them. The history of their growth rates is hidden beneath the bark. During each growing season of its life, the tree adds a measure of new wood to its core of standing timber. The only way to determine the tree's growth rate over time is to count and measure each ring of heartwood and sapwood. (It is not necessary to fell the tree to examine the inside, but it helps.) Ninety-three sugar maples, yellow birches, American beeches, mountain maples, and red spruces of average vigor were felled, examined, measured, weighed, chopped up, and analyzed. No part of the trees was overlooked—roots that could not be pulled up were blasted out of the ground for study. The trees were taken from all elevations at Hubbard Brook, representing all age classes including very old trees that the loggers had overlooked. Wood cores were bored from another 497 representative trees, and their heights and diameters recorded throughout the forest. The scope and extent of the data generated by Likens and Bormann at Hubbard Brook were virtually unparalleled. What they found was astounding.

The ten oldest trees, which predated the Revolutionary War, showed steady growth from 1760 to 1890, the year that the rest

Field study on diseased tree roots. Source: USDA Forest Service.

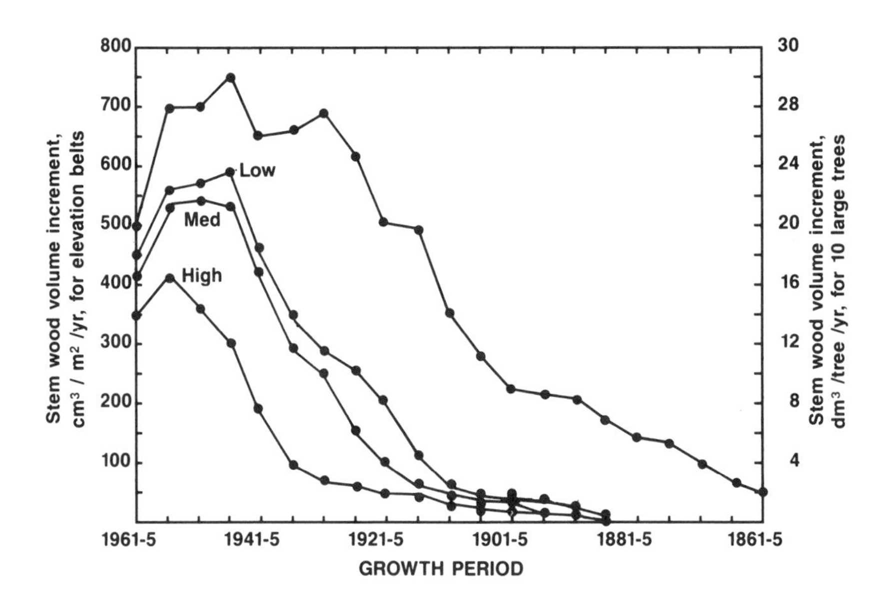

Fig. 4 — Patterns of Tree Growth.

Patterns of stem wood volume growth for Hubbard Brook forest, based on analysis of volume increments by 5-yr periods. The upper curve shows mean volume growth for 10 large trees, in $dm^3/tree/year$ as indicated on the right ordinate. The three lower curves show total forest volume growth by trees now living for the three elevation belts, in $cm^3/m^2/yr$ as indicated on the left ordinate. Source: R.H. Whittaker, F.H. Bormann, G.E. Likens, and T.G. Siccama, The Hubbard Brook Ecosystem Study: Forest Biomass and Production, *Ecological Monographs,* Vol 44, No. 2 (1974).

of the trees studied began to appear. From 1890 to 1910, when the logging began, trees of all age groups, types and elevations showed continual gradual growth. After about 1910, the forest began to show the strong and steady growth rate expected of a young, recently cut forest. From 1910 to 1950, the trees grew at an exponential rate, a rate of rapid growth that Likens and Bormann believed should have continued for many decades. Instead, however, the accelerated growth rate came to an end in the early 1950s. From 1950 to 1960, the growth rate of trees below 2,300 feet either flattened out or actually began to decline. The growth rate of the forest as a whole declined 18 percent from 1950 to 1960. Trees above the 2,300-foot elevation continued to exhibit strong growth until about 1960, in part because they were younger than the trees below. After 1960, however, trees of all sizes, kinds, and at all elevations showed an abrupt and striking decrease in growth and productivity. (See Figure 4.) The growth rate of the sugar maples was 29.7 percent lower from 1961 to 1965 than it had been from 1956 to 1960. For yellow birch the decline was 26.8 percent, for American beech 24.1 percent, and for mountain maple 16.2 percent. The greatest decline of all, however, was experienced by the red spruce—60.2 percent. Moreover, since 1945, there had been only limited tree reproduction in the forest.

The correlation between the decline of this forest and the onset of modern air pollution was strong. In the early 1950s, when man-made pollution caused the precipitation in the Northeast to become unnaturally acidic, the young sugar maples, yellow birches, and American beeches at Hubbard Brook abruptly halted their accelerating rates of growth. As the air pollution worsened over the next ten years, the trend of growth of the trees reversed and sharply declined. The hearty, relatively younger red spruces continued to exhibit strong growth until 1960, when they began to succumb. Moreover, the trees most vulnerable to air pollution injury, the high-elevation red spruces, suffered the severest decline of all.

The picture was complicated by the fact that the years 1961 to 1965 were marked by drought. For ten years after Likens and Bormann completed their work in 1974, scientists would argue whether the decline at Hubbard Brook had been triggered by the drought or by the worsening air pollution. However, the evidence proved that the growth of the trees had been interrupted in the early 1950s, years before the arrival of the drought. Moreover, there had undoubtedly been many severe droughts since 1760, but none of them had had an appreciable effect on the trees before the age of acid rain.

Two scientists, Dr. R. H. Whittaker of Cornell University and Dr. Thomas G. Siccama of Yale University, had helped Likens and Bormann with their comprehensive study at Hubbard Brook. In 1974, the year these four scientists announced their startling findings, nearly 50 million tons of sulfur dioxide and nitric oxide gases were added to the air in the United States. The predictions were that it would continue to get worse as increasing amounts of fossil fuels continued to be burned annually. Likens, Bormann and the others published their findings of forest decline jointly in *Ecological Monographs*:

The decrease was not only abrupt but intense (with wood volume growth reduced by 18% 1956-60). 1961-65 was a period of both drought and increasing acidity of rainfall from air pollution by sulfur and nitrogen oxides from industry in the northeastern United States (Likens *et al.* 1972). Reduction of forest production by acidity of rain has been suggested (Bolin 1971). The history of wood volume growth for the Hubbard Brook forests, which in some trees can be followed for more than two centuries, records no previous decrease in growth such as occurred in 1961-1965. The decrease consequently suggests an anomaly of forest function in the present period of increasingly widespread pollution. The decrease is deserving of further study.[4]

Out of Hubbard Brook had come a most serious warning: that the "anomaly of forest function" occurring there might very well be happening throughout all the great forests of northern New York and New England where exposure to air pollution was equally chronic. Fortunately, scattered throughout the North were several fine universities with students and professors willing to devote their careers to the complex and demanding science of forestry. The warning would not go unheeded.

During his earliest years at Hubbard Brook, Siccama had been one of Vogelmann's graduate students at the University of Vermont. While majoring in forest ecology, he showed enormous energy and commitment, learning everything he could about the ecosystem on Camels Hump, the crown jewel of the Green Mountains. From 1963 to 1968, under Vogelmann's guidance, Siccama exhaustively studied the soils, climate, and vegetation of the mountain from the lowly mosses to the towering trees. He made several hundred trips up Camels Hump, and innumerable trips up other mountains both north and south of it as well. In 1968 he produced a two volume thesis, "Altitudinal Distribution of Forest Vegetation in Relation to Soil and Climate on the Slopes of Green Mountains". The thesis helped earn his doctorate from the University of Vermont and a position on the faculty of the Yale School of Forestry and Environmental Studies. Years later, Vogelmann said that Siccama's work "established a detailed data base that is of incalculable value today."[5] Another professor at the University of Vermont, Dr. Richard M. Klein, called Siccama's work ". . . the only decent data base for a natural area that exists in the world . . ."[6] for this type of forest research.

Siccama knew from the start that the problem of forest decline was not limited to Hubbard Brook. As early as 1963, during a period of severe drought in the Northeast, he had found a high rate of mortality in the red spruce stands on Camels Hump. Trees of all ages had succumbed, and the deaths continued during the remaining years of his graduate work. From 1969 to 1980 Siccama, Vogelmann, and Margaret Bliss, a botany student from the University of Vermont, conducted a series of follow-up studies of the trees on the Green Mountains-Camels Hump and three of its neighbors, Mt. Abraham to the south, and Bolton Mountain and Jay Peak to the north. These four mountains lie along a ridge that extends through Vermont like a backbone, sixty miles from central Vermont to the Canadian border. By gathering additional data in 1969, 1971, 1979, and 1980 from the same forty-three stands that Siccama had been studying since 1963, these researchers compiled seventeen years of comparative information with which to determine the extent of the decline, its intensity, and its duration.

By focusing their attention on the Green Mountains, Siccama, Vogelmann, and Bliss could study the extensive, mature forests of the Northeast. This type of forest was not available to the scientists at Hubbard Brook, because all of the study area had been logged at one time or another. On Camels Hump, however, there were tracts of both cut and uncut forests. In about 1870, the selective logging of red spruce trees had taken place below the 2,600-foot elevation. The selective cutting of yellow birch and sugar maple also occurred in the lower elevations in the mid-1950s. Above 2,600 feet on Camels Hump, logging had been limited. The forests there had never been developed; therefore, there were no ski areas on the mountain or homes above 2,600 feet. The only visible signs of man in the boreal zone were the hiking trails, the twisted remains of a World War II military aircraft which had crashed there, and the charred foundation of a long-abandoned summit house.

The Green Mountains offered the scientists opportunities to expand on the work done at Hubbard Brook. Likens and Bormann had suggested that the trees at the highest elevations, particularly red spruce, were more severely affected than lower-elevation hardwoods. Since the Hubbard Brook study area did not extend above 2,600 feet, they had been unable to follow-up on that lead. Scientists at the University of Vermont, on the other hand, had access to slopes at all elevations on the Green Mountains because the State of Vermont owned them, and the State Department of Forests, Parks, and Recreation gave the university permission to study the area.

Woodcut published in the 1850s, illustrating a typical New England sawmill and logging camp. Such enterprises contributed significantly to early American economy. Source: USDA Forest Service.

In addition, there were substantial age differences between the two forests. The trees at Hubbard Brook were generally quite young; the handful of older trees there were only about 200 years old in the early 1960s. The forests in the Green Mountains, however, were generally much older, and above 3,000 feet there were many spruces older than 300 years old—the oldest spruce that Siccama found there was more than 350 years old.

Siccama, Bliss, and Vogelmann gathered detailed data from hundreds of red spruces, sugar maples, American beeches, white birches, balsam firs, and other trees growing at elevations from 1,800 to 3,800 feet on the four mountains. They studied a variety of vital signs including seedling reproduction, density of living and dead stems, and amount of standing wood. In addition, Siccama took cores in 1964, 1971, and 1980 from forty-seven large red spruces in the lower boreal zone on Camels Hump between 3,000 and 3,400 feet, so that he could study the progress of the trees over time. The information generated by these studies gave a clear and frightening picture of the condition of the Green Mountain forests.

The data showed that since at least 1965 the forests on the four mountains had suffered widespread, substantial, and sustained decrease in growth. Furthermore, the growth rates of red spruce and other trees had declined so severely that they were dying prematurely by the thousands. From 1965 to 1979 the sugar maple, striped maple, mountain maple, mountain ash, and American beech trees fared worst in the very zones where they should have been growing best, at elevations below 2,500 feet. The amount of living sugar maple wood there declined by 16 percent; the amount of striped maple by 24 percent; mountain maple by 57 percent; mountain ash by 17 percent; and American beech by 30 percent. Even more alarming was the deterioration of sugar maple reproduction. Sugar maple is by far the most important tree in the hardwood zone. During that same brief period, the number of sugar maple saplings and seedlings declined by 57 percent. In fact, only one lower-elevation tree, the yellow birch, showed a gain since 1965.

The decline of the red spruce in the boreal zone, however, was far more severe. Two centuries earlier, more than half of the trees above 2,200 feet on Camels Hump were red spruce, but by 1979 red spruce comprised only 10 to 20 percent of the high-elevation stands. The decline of the red spruce in the northern Green Mountains began about 1960, at the same time red spruces started to decline in the White Mountains of New Hampshire. The worst of the decline, however, came later. From 1964 to 1979 nearly half of the red spruces on Camels Hump died—there had been a 43 percent decline in the amount of standing red spruce wood. In 1979, more of the spruce wood on Camels Hump was dead than alive. Although the decline was most pronounced among the oldest trees, young red spruces were not exempted. Trees of all ages, sizes, and at various elevations succumbed on all four mountains, while the rate of seedling reproduction declined by about 50 percent.

Microscopic examination of the growth rings from affected tree cores revealed what had happened. As trees slowly lost vigor, their growth rates declined. When the trees were no longer able to produce more than two-thirds of a millimeter of new wood per year, they died. All forty-seven of the red spruces cored by Siccama in the boreal zone of Camels Hump between 1964 and 1980 suffered this fate. The fifteen trees cored in 1964 could not be cored again in 1971, because they died in the interim, their growth rates being below two-thirds of a millimeter per year from 1959 to 1964. The twenty-one spruces cored in 1971 produced nearly a millimeter of new wood per year from 1959 to 1964; however, their growth rates declined to below the critical level from 1964 to 1971. By

Forest ranger studies a core from an increment boring taken to determine age of trees and their rate of growth. Source: USDA Forest Service.

the time they were to be cored again in 1980, they had disappeared. The eleven spruces cored in 1980 grew well up to 1964, at a rate of well over a millimeter per year; yet, by 1980 they too declined to the point of no return.

As the red spruce progressively died out over almost twenty years, the balsam fir, its chief competitor above 2,500 feet, got a golden opportunity to take over the growing spaces defaulted by the dead spruces. The fragrant firs on Camels Hump, on average much younger that the red spruces, should have filled the void aggressively. Although the firs generally appeared to be healthy, they did not respond to the spruce decline with the expected vigor. Samples of ring growth taken from fir cores showed that they had declined too; from 1965 to 1979 the amount of living balsam fir wood declined by 6 percent. Unusually large numbers of dead balsam firs were found on Camels Hump. The volume of standing white birch, the only other tree that can live in the boreal zone, increased by 15 percent.

The signs Siccama, Bliss, and Vogelmann saw in the Green Mountains indicated that the massive decline of red spruce was not only continuing but accelerating. They travelled to other parts of central and northern New England, to the Adirondacks of New York, and to the White Mountains of New Hampshire to look at other forests, to talk to other scientists, and to determine whether the problem was unique to Vermont. It was not. The decline was region-wide and becoming worse. They were told that red spruce was dying in the Adirondacks at about the same order of magnitude as it was declining in Vermont. At Hubbard Brook in the White Mountains, the density of red spruce saplings declined by nearly 80 percent between 1965 and 1977, and the number of large spruces declined by more than 50 percent. No spruce seedlings were found at Hubbard Brook in 1965 or in 1977.

The correlation between forests declining and modern air pollution was strong. The regional signs of declining growth for red spruce appeared in the early 1960s, shortly after the period associated by Likens and Bormann with the onset of unnaturally acidic precipitation in the Northeast. As the air pollution problem worsened during the following decades, the decline of the forests intensified. The devastation was most severe in the high-elevation evergreen forests where exposure to air pollution was most chronic. High-elevation red spruces, young and old, throughout the northern Appalachians displayed the same pattern of death: their foliage turned brown and died from the top down and from the outside in. In most locations, many more spruces died on the windward westerly slopes of mountains than on the less-directly exposed easterly slopes. The signs of decline that appeared in the wood of the trees before the severe drought of the early 1960s continued unabated long after the drought ended. The only region where the red spruce still appeared to be healthy was in the southern Appalachian mountains, which had not been subjected to the same intensely acidic precipitation that the northern Appalachians had been receiving since the early 1950s.

Siccama, Bliss, and Vogelmann summed up their findings with characteristic scientific understatement in an article published in 1982 in the *Bulletin of the Torrey Botanical Club*:

The broad scale decline of red spruce is especially significant in terms of its present population trends relative to its presumed importance in the presettlement virgin forests of the region. Historically the virgin forests of the lower and mid slopes of the mountains of New England had sufficient red spruce to support a major forestry base. A whole network of railroads and mills in the White Mountains was established for the harvesting of red spruce timber from the late 1800s to the 1920s. A mill for the production of spruce wood products, especially butter boxes, existed in the valley adjacent to our study area on

Camels Hump . . . The decline of this long lived shade tolerant conifer over a major part of its regional range (slopes of the New England mountains) is not the anticipated pattern based on its known ecological strategies and presumed former abundance.[7]

Declining stand of red spruce on Camels Hump. Source: Author's collection.

Nearly twenty years of intensive, independent field work and research by several highly qualified scientists produced by 1980 substantial evidence that air pollution was closely associated with the decline of great forests in the Northeast. Some scientists, including Vogelmann and Klein at the University of Vermont, believed that the evidence justified the conclusion that air pollution was the probable cause of the decline. An array of industry officials, government agency representatives, and others, however, either refused to draw that inference or argued that more certainty was required before anyone should be compelled to bear the expense of curing the problem. On the other hand, Siccama and other scientists were not convinced that the case against air pollution had yet been made; they believed that the correlation between air pollution and forest decline might turn out to be merely a coincidence and that some other, as yet unidentified force, could be the cause. Industry benefitted from a division of opinion in the scientific community.

By 1982 the debate over air pollution had polarized American scientists. While this was chiefly the natural result of honest scientific disagreement about a complex environmental problem, the controversy also had a parochial element. In that same year, the American Chemical Society held a symposium on acid rain, one aspect of air pollution. After listening for several days to speeches by scientists on both sides of the issue, Ms. Bette Hileman, a representative of the Society, summed up the status of the debate in an article published by *Environmental Science & Technology* in 1982:

> . . . [C]ontroversy envelops almost all aspects of the acid rain issue. Informed individuals, including most of the scientists who study the problem, have divided into two opposing groups. A reason for this polarity may be found in the composition of the two groups: those who live in regions that may be harmed by delaying acid rain controls, and those who enjoy the economic benefits of further delay. Thomas D. Crocker of the University of Wyoming expressed this idea when he said: "Opponents of control, those to whom the expected net benefits of control are negative, insist that more information is required before 'rational' control decisions can be made. . . . On the other hand, proponents, those to whom the expected net benefits of control are positive, fear the possible environmental effects of delay—they want control now." Currently, there are 10 bills before Con-

gress that address the issue of acid rain. Polarization over this subject is so extreme that it is probable no action will be taken on the bills.[8]

While people debated the issue, Vogelmann, Klein, and several other prominent scientists set out to find the definitive evidence, the smoking gun that would prove whether the correlation was significant or merely coincidental, causal or casual. From this point on, Vogelmann and Siccama would go their separate ways.

Fig. 5 — *Picea rubens.*

Source: USDA Forest Service.

4

Discovering Invisible Pathways

In 1979 Vogelmann and Klein set up within the Botany Department at the University of Vermont the Acidic Deposition Research Project to research the effects of acidic precipitation and fallout on terrestrial ecosystems. Together with two of their research scientists, Tim Scherbatskoy and Margaret Bliss, they hoped to discover the invisible pathways by which air pollution could cause the visible signs of death and decline in the forests.

The team believed that there were several broad avenues through which air pollution could be harming the trees: through direct action on the foliage, through indirect attack through the soil, or through both. Since the corrosive effects of acid rain on statues and buildings had been well documented for some time, it was possible that it could have a related effect on plants. If acids from the air could dissolve stone structures and eat away at a variety of metals, perhaps the acids could also cause direct injury to the living tissues of trees. Furthermore, as the acids percolated through the soil and combined with the various chemicals there, the roots of the trees could be poisoned or otherwise harmed. The effects of acid precipitation on high-elevation forest soils could be most profound during spring runoff. The peaks of the northern Appalachian Mountains are commonly under snow cover for five out of the twelve months. A sudden surge of huge quantities of pollutants and acids in the springtime, just as most of the trees are awakening from winter dormancy, could give a toxic shock to young, new roots. During one early spring runoff on Camels Hump, Vogelmann and Klein found that the meltwater had a pH of 3.1.

Forest researcher measures the size of the needles and the growth rate as judged by the distance between twigs on a branchlet cut from the lower third of the crown.
Source: USDA Forest Service.

The Acidic Deposition Research Project team would explore both the foliage and the soils for evidence to substantiate these theories. The group would also look beyond acidic deposition to explore the effects that other pollutants in the air might have on the forests. This team of scientists had important resources not readily available to most others—immediate access to the severely stressed high-elevation forests and an excellent laboratory where field specimens and observations could be analyzed and tested. In Vogelmann and Klein, they gained expertise in two complementary areas. Vogelmann had spent his career in the field mastering the art of close and thorough observation of symptoms; while Klein's training and experience had made him as adept in the lab as Vogelmann was in the field.

Klein was a plant physiologist, a botanist specializing in the functions and vital processes of living plants. After earning his doctorate in both botany and biochemistry from the University of Chicago in 1951, Klein spent fourteen years at the prestigious New York Botanical Garden, serving first as an assistant curator, then as associate curator, and finally as the A. H. Caspary Curator of Plant Physiology from 1958 to 1967. He has written or co-authored three books on botany and edited several others. More than one hundred research papers in scientific journals bear his name, and he managed to find time to write another 90 articles for popular gardening magazines and other publications.

Klein is a scientist's scientist. He has served as Chairman of the American Society for Plant Physiology (Northeast Section), and has been appointed to the Councils of the Botanical Society of America, the Society for Economic Botany, the American Society for Photobiology, and the Developmental Biology Society. He was chosen editor of the *Plant Science Bulletin*, associate editor of the *Botanical Review*, and member of the editorial boards of *Economic Botany* and *Environmental and Experimental Botany*. At the University of Vermont, the laboratories of the Botany Department are under his supervision and control. His expertise in both theory and experimental technique would enable him to analyze field observations in the laboratory and suggest new areas to explore. The team of Vogelmann and Klein brought a unique blend of field and laboratory experience to the project, one which would be difficult to rival in diagnosing accurately the destructive forces at work on the red spruce.

Much of the scientific research before 1979 probing the effects of air pollution focused on foliage. Each needle and leaf of a tree is a living factory designed, like a man-made factory, to take in raw products, convert them into finished products through a manufacturing process, and dispose of waste products. Through photosynthesis, respiration, and other miraculous processes, the foliage of a tree is able to convert minerals into the carbohydrates, sugars, proteins, amino acids, and other organic substances necessary for life and growth. The key to this process is the leaf's chlorophyll. (See Figure 6.) Most of the required raw products needed by the leaf, like calcium, magnesium, and potassium, are supplied to it by the tree through the soil. Other required substances, like carbon dioxide and nitrogen, come from the air, and still others, like moisture, come from both the soil and the air. Through the innumerable microscopic pores on its surface, each needle and leaf is able to take in essential gases and water vapors from the air; it then returns to the air that precious waste product of photosynthesis, oxygen. Each of the pores is housed within a skin-like epidermis which, in turn, is covered by a delicate, waxy coating that protects it from disease and from premature dehydration.

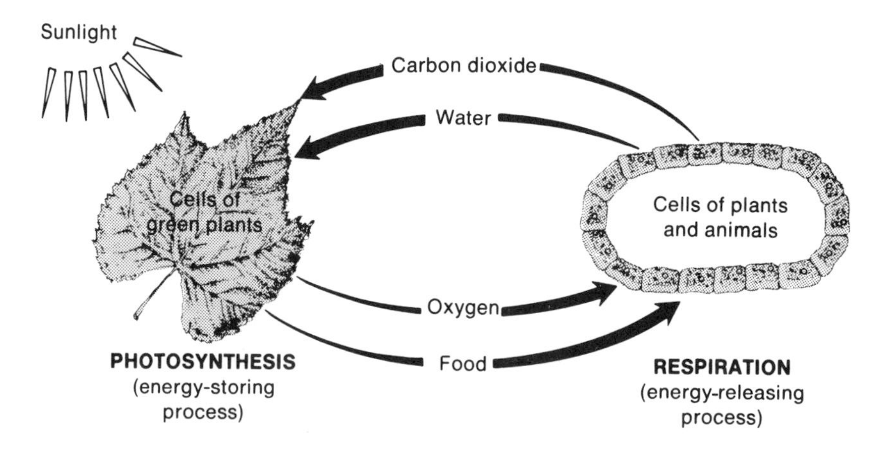

Fig. 6 — Photosynthesis and Respiration

By 1979, scientists recognized two ways in which air pollution could cause direct harm to the foliage of trees. One pathway enabled poisonous gases to penetrate the interior of a leaf or needle, and the other involved destruction of its protective exterior. Since a function of foliage is to exchange gases and vapors with the air, poisonous gases like sulfur dioxide, nitric oxide, nitrogen dioxide, and ozone were known to penetrate leaves and needles and to damage vital cells. When, for example, sulfur dioxide is absorbed into the needles of evergreens, it comes into contact with moist, reactive surfaces of mesophyll and palisade cells and turns into sulfite—sulfite is very toxic to cells and will quickly kill them if present in sufficiently high concentrations. Different chemical reactions occur when the other poisonous gases enter the needles, but the result is the same: the destruction of chlorophyll and other substances essential to photosynthesis. As the levels of chlorophyll in the foliage drop, the tree must rely more and more upon the carbohydrates, proteins and other building blocks of life stored in its older needles if the tree is to continue to grow. As more and more older needles begin to yellow, turn brown prematurely, die and fall, the tree's stores of carbohydrates and other forms of energy are reduced, and so is its capacity to replace them through photosynthesis. As the tree gradually weakens, its new needles get shorter and shorter, its growth rate slows, its roots die back, and the tree loses its vigor. If the concentrations of pollutants are high enough, or if the exposures are long enough, the tree may die. Ever since the early 1940s, scientists had been documenting the destruction of forests located near power plants, factories, and smelters that emitted large quantities of these poisonous gases.

In addition, the evergreen tree must also cope with the leaching of its foliage by the acids in precipitation. As early as the 1880s, scientists already suspected that normal rainwater, fog, and dew, which could erode and corrode rock, were also washing away mineral nutrients from the foliage of trees. It took the discovery of radioisotopes in the twentieth century, however, to prove it. In the 1950s, the pioneers in the study of foliar leaching, Dr. H. B. Tukey of Michigan State University and his son, Dr. H. B. Tukey, Jr. of Cornell University, performed experiments in which they allowed laboratory plants to take up radioactive forms of nutrients, like calcium, magnesium, and potassium, through their roots. Since these minerals were radioactive, their progress through the plants could be followed.

The Tukeys found that surprisingly large amounts of the mineral nutrients were washed out of the leaves by distilled, nonacidic water. In subsequent years they and other scientists, using improved techniques, found that significant quantities of all the common inorganic nutrients, plus organic materials such as amino acids, sugars, and carbohydrates, were leached out of the foliage of a variety of plants by simulated rain and fog made up of neutral water. They found that the amount of material leached depended upon a number of conditions, such as the amount available in the leaves, the amount of sunlight the plant received, the age of the leaves, and their general condition. The advent of unnaturally acidic precipitation added a new condition to the list, a condition for which evolution had not prepared the trees. During the decades following the Tukeys' work, scientists became increasingly concerned that acidic precipitation was damaging the waxy coating that protect needles and leaves from drying out, and was now leaching nutrients from the foliage of trees at such an accelerated rate that the trees were no longer able to maintain adequate supplies of nutrients in their foliage.

Likens and Bormann, once again at the forefront of forest research, had been among the first scientists in the United States to discover that modern air pollution was having a discernible effect on the foliage of forests far removed from heavily populated, industrialized centers. From June to October of 1969, together with a colleague, John S. Eaton of Cornell University, they studied the extent to which rain was removing nutrients from the foliage, stems, and bark of sugar maple, yellow birch, and American beech trees at Hubbard Brook in the White Mountains. These were the same trees they subsequently found to have been declining in productivity since the early 1950s. The pH of the precipitation was an acidic 4.06 during the study; sulfate and nitrate accounted for 85 percent of the negatively charged ions in the rain. As the rain hit the trees and percolated through the leaves, it was collected by the scientists and analyzed for the presence of certain nutrient elements. They found that the acidic rain had leached potassium, magnesium, calcium, phosphorus, and other nutrients from the trees at a faster rate than normal. They also found extremely large amounts of sulfur in the rainfall collected under the trees. Their follow-up studies at Hubbard Brook convinced them that the excessive amounts of sulfur had come from airborne sulfur dioxide gas deposited on, and absorbed by, the leaves and by sulfur particles impacted onto the leaves by the winds.

Eaton, Likens, and Bormann published their findings in 1973 in the *Journal of Ecology*:

> The additional leaching by this more acid rain may be one of the indirect effects of air pollution on terrestrial ecosystems. Although SO_4 and NO_3 in the atmosphere may be derived from both natural and man-made sources, the importance of the relationship between the acidification of rain by man-made pollutants and the mechanism of leaching by hydrogen-ion exchange takes on added significance and must become the subject of intense study.[1]

In addition to studying the scientific work done before 1979, the Acidic Deposition Research Project also followed current work of scientists in Europe and North America. On both continents, scientists discovered that the foliage of declining trees contained approximately 10 percent more sulfur than the foliage of healthy trees. One of the most important studies of the chemistry of red spruce foliage on Camels Hump was done by Deborah G. Lord, a graduate student at the University of Pennsylvania. She studied the foliage of declining and healthy red spruce trees at various elevations on the mountain. She found that the higher up the mountain she went, the higher the concentrations were of sulfur and nitrogen in the needles of the trees. More important, at every elevation trees with visible signs of decline had substantially higher concentrations of sulfur in their needles than did the healthy-looking red spruces. Lord discovered something else of significance—at the higher elevations where the decline of the red spruce was most severe, and where the trees were subjected to the highest amounts of acidic precipitation, there was less potassium in the needles of the red spruces than there was at the lower elevations.

Lord's discoveries were consistent with both branches of the theory that air pollution could harm the foliage of remote forest trees: that poisonous gases (sulfur and nitrogen oxides) would get into the foliage and destroy the chlorophyll, and that the acidic precipitation would strip important nutrients (potassium) from the foliage at a faster rate than the trees could cope with. Scherbatskoy and Klein decided to follow up on these findings with field and laboratory studies of their own.

In the laboratory, Scherbatskoy and Klein performed two separate experiments, one with yellow birch and white spruce seedlings and the other using red spruce seedlings. The experiments were to determine whether seedlings misted with water acidified to pH 4.3 would lose any more potassium or other important substances than would seedlings misted with water at pH 5.6, the pH of normal rainwater before the early 1950s. They found that the foliage of the spruces lost more potassium, carbohydrates, and proteins when misted with water at pH 4.3 than they did at pH

5.6. The yellow birches also lost more vital substances at the lower pH, although their losses were not as great as those of the red spruces. When Scherbatskoy and Klein measured the acidity of the moisture that fell from the foliage of the birch and spruce seedlings, they found that it had lost some of its acidity. They concluded that the acids in the water had reacted chemically with the tissues of the foliage to cause the leaching of potassium and the other vital substances.

Scherbatskoy supplemented these laboratory studies with field observations to see whether the process that had occurred in the lab occurred in the forest. The results were similar. He found that the precipitation that fell through the red spruce canopy was enriched in potassium, calcium, nitrates, and sulfate, and that some of the acidity of the precipitation had been absorbed by the trees.

These findings were consistent with the results obtained by other scientists doing similar work with sugar maples, American beeches, and other types of forest trees. Collectively they indicated that air pollution was having a measurable and negative effect on the foliage of the forests in the Northeast. There was general agreement among scientists that the growth rates of the forests could be reduced by the combined action of the poisonous gases and the acidic precipitation on the foliage. What was still disputed, however, was whether the measured effects on the foliage alone were serious enough to cause the widespread death and decline that these forests were experiencing. Since no one could yet say how much poisonous gas or acidic precipitation it took to kill a tree, the most a scientist could say was that the damage being done to the foliage was at least a contributing factor to the decline of the forests. If there was a smoking gun to be found, the Acidic Precipitation Research Project would have to search for it in the soil.

Stable soil is one of the most critical components of a tree's environment. Even a small change in the chemistry of the upper twelve inches of soil, where nearly all of a tree's important feeder roots are located, can be profound enough to cause the widespread decline of forest trees. Trees need to obtain from the soil large concentrations of calcium, phosphorus, and potassium, among other things, in order to live. If a conifer cannot get sufficient amounts of any one of these essential nutrients from the soil, its growth rate is suppressed and its foliage turns brown and dies. (See Figure 7.)

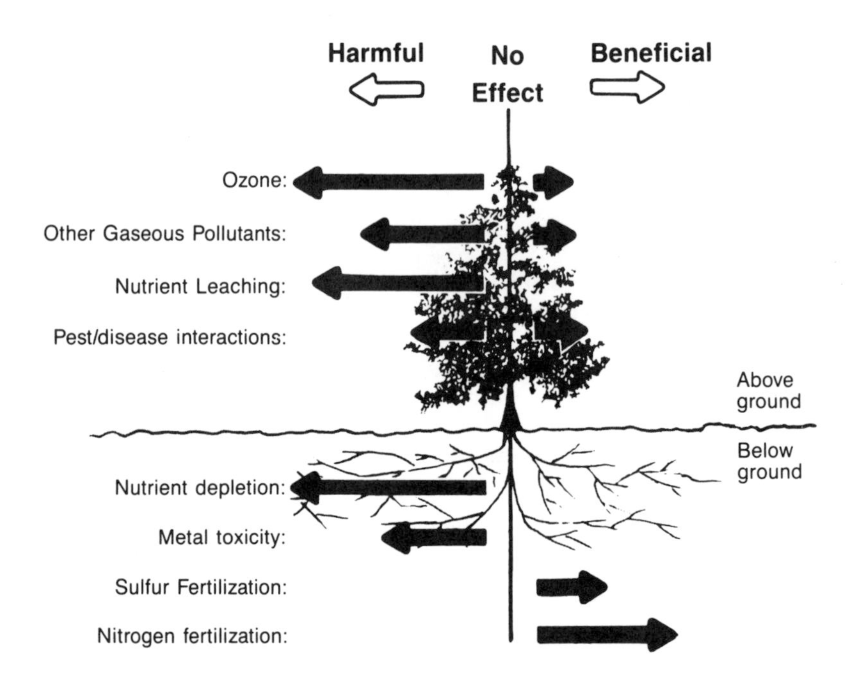

Fig. 7 — Potential Effects of Air Pollutants (acid deposition, ozone, and other gases) on Forest Growth

Source: Office of Technology Assessment, 1984.

Trees compete for nutrients with other trees and plants in the forest, and with natural processes that consume nutrients and wash them away from the soil. As dead leaves and branches on the forest floor decompose and return nutrients to the soil, a number of weak organic and carbonic acids are produced and washed into the soil by natural rainwater, which itself is slightly acidic. Minerals such as calcium neutralize these natural acids and serve as a buffer preventing the soil from becoming too acidic. When minerals are used up this way, however, they are no longer available as food for the trees; they are either converted into chemical compounds that cannot be taken up by the roots, or they are washed away from the roots and into the groundwater.

The thin glacial soils of Camels Hump and the other Green Mountains of Vermont are naturally acidic and lacking in lime at the high elevations. Since the amounts of calcium, magnesium, and potassium needed to support the trees and buffer the soil are severely limited, very few trees can survive in this delicately balanced, uncompromising environment. The red spruce, the balsam fir, and the white birch survive in the boreal zones of these mountains only because they have evolved in a way that enables them to compete efficiently for these nutrients and to keep them tightly recycled. For sixteen years, Dr. Bernhard Ulrich, a soils scientist at the University of Göttingen, conducted intensive studies of the mountain forests in the Harz and Solling regions of West Germany, while following the work of scientists studying forest soils in many countries under differing climatic conditions. He concluded that air pollution was profoundly changing the chemistry of the forest soils, and that these changes were causing the serious decline of the Norway spruce, silver fir, and European beech throughout Europe and Scandinavia. Soil analyses revealed that as the acidity of soils increased, the losses of calcium and other necessary nutrients also increased. The growth rates of seriously damaged spruce and fir trees there had decreased to such an extent that in some cases the annual growth rings were partly missing. Laser spectroscopy showed a reduction of calcium and magnesium in the cell walls of the roots in most damaged trees. Based on these findings, Ulrich theorized that the chronic, long-term accumulation of sulfuric and nitric acids from precipitation and fallout had stripped away important soil nutrients at an accelerated rate, and that the natural process of recycling nutrients through decomposition and weathering did not keep up with the net annual losses. This theory was first proposed by Dr. Lars N. Overrein of the Norwegian Institute for Forest Research, whose early experiments established by 1972 that the losses of calcium from different types of soils increased drastically as the acidity of precipitation increased.

Several scientists studying forest damage in the northeastern United States found symptoms similar to those in the declining forests of West Germany. In 1979, scientists from Syracuse University discovered substantial losses of calcium from conifer sites in the Huntington Forest of the Adirondack Mountains, losses which they attributed to leaching by acid rain. Furthermore, the growth rate of red spruces on those sites had been declining since 1965, and the root systems of the trees had few fine feeder roots embedded in the mineral soil. Other scientists found that for at least eleven years, acid precipitation had been removing substantial amounts of calcium, magnesium, potassium, and sodium from the soils of the Hubbard Brook Experimental Forest; the losses of calcium were twice as high from 1971 to 1974 as they were from 1963 to 1966. More recent studies at the University of Maine demonstrated that acid rain was leaching away calcium, magnesium, potassium, and other nutrients from soils on the high elevation fir forests in the Green Mountains north and south of Camels Hump. Moreover, another study concerning the foliage and the roots of red spruce in Vermont and New Hampshire, conducted at the University of Pennsylvania, revealed abnormally low levels of calcium in the roots of declining stands of red spruce trees on Camels Hump.

Vogelmann and Klein believed that these findings justified the conclusion that man-made air pollution was changing the balance of natural forest soils in the Northeast by depleting the stores of essential nutrients. This process could explain why red spruce trees were dying in large numbers on the high-elevation slopes of the Green Mountains. It could not, however, explain why red spruce trees were also dying at lower elevations where the forest soils still had ample concentrations of calcium and other nutrients. Although fewer trees were dying there than at the higher elevations, something else was probably contributing to the overall decline. Klein decided to investigate another, more controversial aspect of Ulrich's acid rain theory.

Ulrich believed that acid precipitation and fallout caused a second kind of change in the chemistry of the forest soils in Europe: the accelerated mobilization of toxic aluminum. Aluminum, an inorganic mineral resource, exists abundantly in soils, but always in combination with other chemicals that make it insoluble. Ulrich theorized that as polluted air and precipitation made the soil more and more acidic, chemical reactions occurred, releasing free aluminum ions from the aluminum hydroxide and other aluminum-bearing compounds of the soil. This free aluminum, which dissolves in water at low pH, poisons plants when absorbed by the roots. Its toxicity depends upon the amount of calcium in the soil. Too much aluminum kills the young feeder roots that supply the tree with water and important nutrients like calcium. If this happens, the tree's water absorbtion is reduced, causing the moisture content of the tree to be abnormally low even where there is adequate soil moisture. The tree's needles or leaves discolor and fall prematurely, its twigs and branches wither and die back, the crown deteriorates, the tree's growth rate slows, and the tree gradually dies over a period that can last several years.

Ulrich based these conclusions on significant changes that had occurred in the soil chemistry of the Solling forests since 1966. The concentrations of soluble aluminum in the soil substantially increased from 1966 to 1978. At the same time, there was a nearly parallel decrease in the amount of fine root tissue during the growing season of the sick and dying trees. Ulrich's studies also revealed that the concentrations of aluminum found in the soil of the forests were in excess of one milligram per liter, a level that could be expected to seriously damage the root systems of the trees. A Swedish scientist, Dr. J. R. Erichsen-Jones, established the relationship between increasing acidity and the effects of aluminum on fish in 1939; Ulrich was the first scientist in Europe to propose that acid precipitation was also killing forests by mobilizing toxic aluminum in the soil. His theory stirred up a great deal of controversy in the scientific community.

Scientists in Canada, however, independently confirmed the validity of the aluminum theory. Sudbury, Ontario, has one of the world's largest deposits of nickel and copper ore. Until 1972, three huge smelters operated a few miles outside the city. Each year they smelted enormous amounts of high-sulfur ore and, in the process, poured more sulfur dioxide into the atmosphere than any other complex in the world. In 1972 more than 3 million tons of sulfur dioxide gas spewed from the stacks of the Sudbury smelters. To make matters worse, many thousands of tons of heavy metals such as nickel, copper, lead, and zinc were also emitted into the air from the smelting process. Large areas of the boreal forests in the region suffered widespread destruction from the pollution. Downwind from the smelters, 160 square miles of trees and vegetation were destroyed, and the remaining soil eroded, leaving nothing but blackened rocks.

Dr. Thomas C. Hutchinson, Professor of Botany at the University of Toronto and Associate Director of the University's Institute for Environmental Studies, analyzed the effects of the sulfur dioxide and the heavy metals on the soils of the Sudbury region from 1970 to 1972. Hutchinson and his colleague, Dr. L.M. Whitby, found that the soils were highly acidic (ranging in pH from 3.8 to 5.2) and toxic to most plants over a very wide area. They did not, however, expect to find unusual levels of aluminum in the soil, since aluminum was not one of the metals given off in the smelting process. Nevertheless, they found highly toxic concentrations of aluminum in the Sudbury soils; the more acidic the soil, the more toxic aluminum they found. The roots of plants they tried to grow near the smelters became deformed with blackened tips, with death following within a few weeks. In a subsequent series of laboratory experiments, Hutchinson and others showed that a nutrient solution containing only 5 milligrams per liter of aluminum was sufficient to inhibit the growth of roots on red spruce seedlings. This indicated that red spruce might be a species sensitive to elevated levels of aluminum in the soil. Hutchinson and Whitby reported their findings in an article published in 1977 by *Water, Air, and Soil Pollution*:

> Aluminum toxicity is apparently caused by highly acidic rainfall mobilizing Al [aluminum] from clay minerals in the Sudbury soils. This effect was unforeseen and may well be a salutary warning for those concerned with acidic rainfall problems on ecosystems both aquatic and terrestrial, in Scandinavia and in the eastern United States.[2]

In 1972 one of the smelters was shut down, and the world's tallest smokestack (1,250 feet) was installed at another to assure that the poisonous emissions would thereafter be carried by the

Smokestacks of Sudbury nickle smelters. Source: Inco, Ltd., Ontario, Canada.

winds far from the Sudbury region. Several years later, another scientist tried adding ground limestone (which is mostly calcium carbonate) to the soil in a semibarren area near a smelter. As a result of the liming, birch seeds that had remained dormant in the polluted soil began to germinate. Seeds would not germinate, however, when other chemicals like calcium chloride (which would produce the same calcium concentration as limestone) or sodium carbonate (to give the same pH as would limestone) were added to the soil. He concluded that the limestone supplied the missing calcium required for nutrition and at the same time combined with the free aluminum, thus eliminating the toxicity of the soil.

Scientists in the United States quickly followed up on the pioneering aluminum research in Canada and Germany. From 1975 to 1977, Dr. Christopher S. Cronan of Dartmouth College and Dr. Carl L. Schofield of Cornell University conducted two independent studies of two separate mountain ranges in the northeastern United States. Cronan studied the subalpine balsam fir zone located at 4,000 feet on Mt. Moosilauke in the White Mountains of New Hampshire; Schofield studied 219 high elevation lakes in the Adirondack Mountains of New York. Both regions received similar amounts of strongly acidic precipitation, with a mean pH between 4.0 and 4.5. Each researcher found unexpectedly high amounts of dissolved aluminum in the ground and surface waters of the mountains, and in 1979 they published their findings jointly in *Science*.[3]

Cronan found that sulfuric acid from the atmosphere and precipitation had replaced organic and carbonic acids as the dominant acids in the forest soils of New Hampshire and the rest of New England, changing the historical trend of aluminum accumulation in the process. By increasing the acidity of the soils, sulfuric acid caused pronounced leaching of toxic aluminum throughout the soil, with the high concentrations of aluminum he found in the New Hampshire forest continuing to increase with soil depth. Schofield found that the aluminum concentrations in the acidified lakes of the Adirondack Mountains were ten to fifty times higher than concentrations in the more neutral waters where fish still lived. He concluded that the runoff of ground and surface water containing high amounts of acidity and aluminum in a watershed caused lakes in the Adirondacks to become toxic to fish. Both Cronan and Schofield concluded that these increases in aluminum were a modern phenomenon caused by polluted air:

> These results from the higher elevations of the White Mountains and Adirondacks region indicate that soil leaching and mineral weathering by acid precipitation lead to comparatively high concentrations of dissolved aluminum in surface and ground waters. Such increased aluminum concentrations can lead to fish mortality at concentrations of approximately 0.2 mg/liter or higher. . . . Accelerated aluminum leaching may also have implications for soil-forming processes, the health of plant communities, and clay mineralogy.[4]

The dying red spruce trees on the Green Mountains looked as if they were suffering from drought, even though they had normal rainfall and adequate soil moisture. This led Vogelmann and Klein to wonder whether the trees had suffered root damage that affected their ability to absorb water. They collected several root specimens from small red spruce, fir, and white birch trees growing on Camels Hump. The roots of the red spruces did not look as healthy. They were discolored, and many of their young feeder roots were dead. Klein then tried to determine whether aluminum would affect the roots of red spruce trees. In the laboratory, he subjected small birch and red spruce trees to acid water containing small amounts of aluminum. He discovered that the acid conditions and aluminum limited the amount of water that the trees could take up through their roots. The tips of the red spruce roots turned brown, and the trees failed to develop lateral roots. Overall, the small plants in the laboratory soon began to look like the dying spruces in the forests.

By now the members of the Acidic Deposition Research Project strongly suspected aluminum poisoning as an important causal factor in the forest decline. Scherbatskoy suggested taking wood cores from red spruce and sugar maple trees on the mountains to determine whether the amount of aluminum and other metals in the wood had changed appreciably during the period associated with the beginnings of acid rain. Vogelmann and Klein agreed.

Scherbatskoy took sections from red spruce and sugar maple cores dating back to the late 1800s and analyzed them chemically for aluminum and other metals. He found that the amount of aluminum in the wood changed very little from the early 1900s until about 1950. From 1950 onward, however, the aluminum content of the spruce and maple wood increased dramatically; in some samples the concentration of aluminum was three times higher than before. He found the same trend to be true of vanadium, a trace metal given off by the combustion of oil and coal. (See Figures 8 and 9.) The trend of accumulating magnesium, however, revealed that its concentrations had been steadily declining over time.

With this evidence in hand, Vogelmann, Klein and Scherbatskoy believed that they had found the smoking gun. As man-made air pollution soaked the soils of the forest with powerful sulfuric and nitric acids year after year, the stores of calcium, magnesium, and other nutrients in the soil were reduced, while the concentrations of soluble aluminum rose to toxic levels. The slow process of decomposition, and the even slower process of weathering, were unable to keep up with the work of the acids. These conclusions were supported by the work of a graduate student from the University of Maine, who in 1980 had analyzed soils on 14 mountains from Vermont to the Gaspé region of Quebec. He reported that

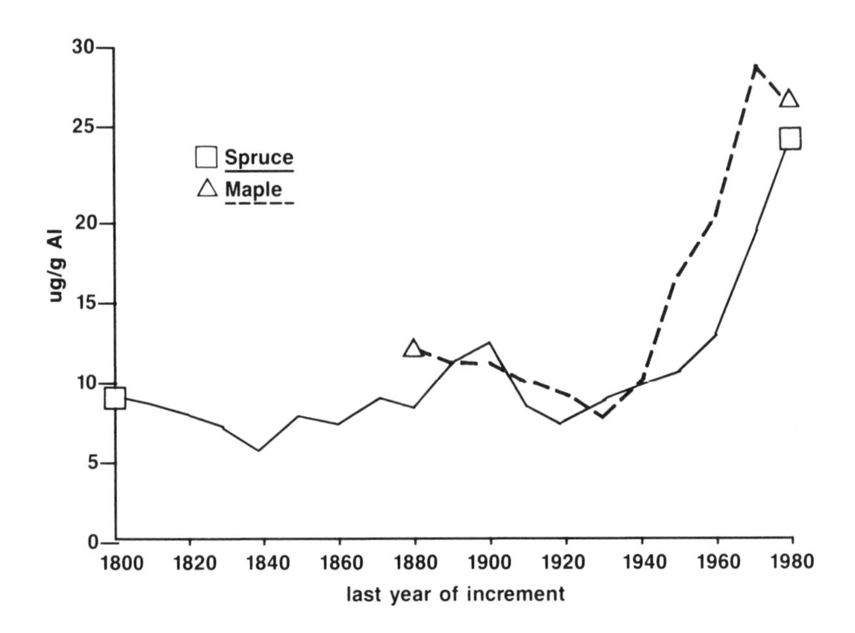

Fig. 8 — Aluminum in Red Spruce and Sugar Maple on Camels Hump.

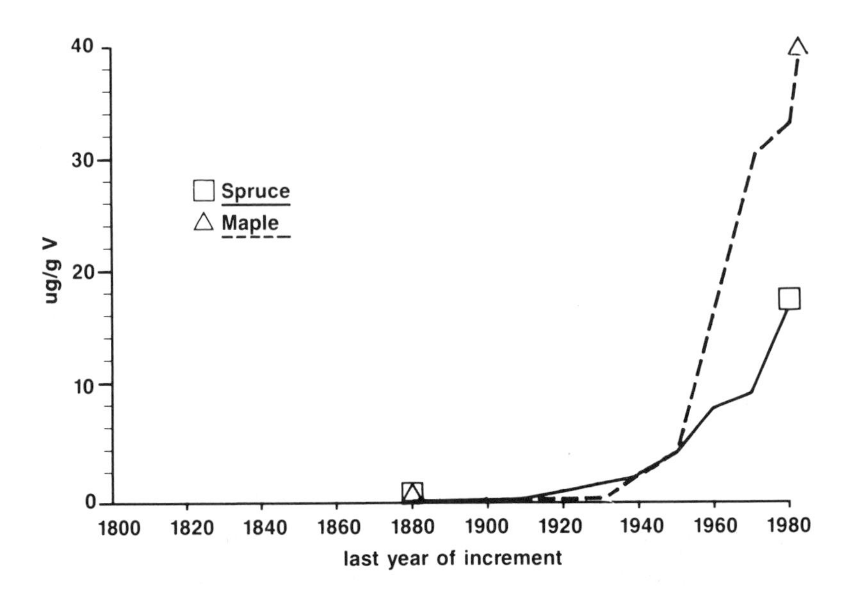

Fig. 9 — Vanadium in Red Spruce and Sugar Maple on Camels Hump.

Source: T. Scherbatskoy, University of Vermont. Based on preliminary data. Reprinted by permission.

the ratio of calcium to aluminum in the soil was only one-fifth of the balance needed for healthy tree growth.

Klein and Vogelmann concluded that the aluminum theory, which Hutchinson and Ulrich had developed in Canada and Germany, was a reality in Vermont. As the levels of soluble aluminum in the soil rose, roots were destroyed, the trees took up less water, their foliage turned brown prematurely and fell, and the trees died. This theory explained why far more trees were dying at the higher elevations than in the lower forests; since the higher elevations were subjected to substantially more acid precipitation and fallout, those soils became more depleted and toxic than those at lower elevations. The theory also explained why red spruce trees were dying in the lower elevations where the soils still contained ample calcium; they also contained toxic aluminum. Unfortunately, it might only be a matter of time before those forests also resembled the embattled boreal zones above.

Toxic levels of aluminum in highly acidic soils alone could be seriously stressing the red spruce. Nevertheless, the Acidic Deposition Research Project suspected that aluminum was probably getting help from its distant cousins, the heavy metals. Lead, copper, zinc, nickel, and cadmium are heavy metallic resources used extensively in industry. They are heavy only in comparison to other elements; for example, cadmium weighs about four time more than aluminum, and lead weighs nearly twice as much as cadmium. Some heavy metals like copper and zinc are called micronutrients—nutrients essential for plants but only in small amounts. Abnormally high concentrations of copper or zinc in the soil can be toxic to trees. The rest of the heavy metals are not

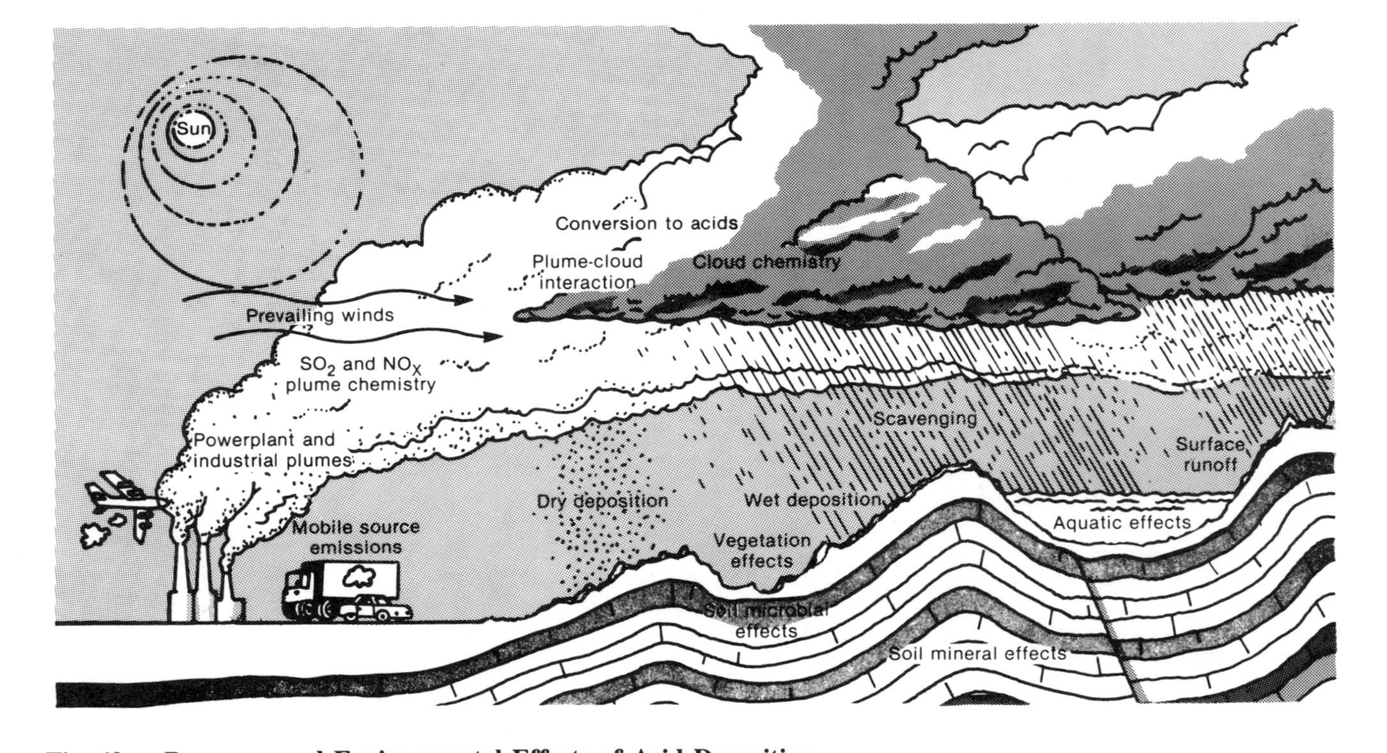

Fig. 10 — Processes and Environmental Effects of Acid Deposition.

Source: Adapted from *The Acid Precipitation Problem* (Corvallis, Oreg.: U.S. Environmental Protection Agency, Environmental Research Laboratory, 1976).

nutrients in any sense of the word; they are pure unalloyed pollutants. Toxic levels of them can change the permeability of plant cell membranes and interfere with the exchange of vital substances.

Lead, copper, zinc, nickel, and cadmium are geochemically scarce metals; forest soils normally contain only trace amounts of each. The high-elevation forests of the Northeast, however, had been accumulating high concentrations of these heavy metals at a rapid rate. The same prevailing winds and storm tracks that bring gases and acids to the eastern United States also bring tons of toxic metallic particles produced by car exhausts and distant industrial smokestacks. The concentrations of copper, lead, and zinc in the floor of the boreal forests on Camels Hump increased dramatically from 1966 to 1980—copper by about 32 percent, lead by 95 percent, and zinc by 48 percent. The concentrations of cadmium found on Camels Hump in 1980 were three times greater than they were in the Solling spruce forests of West Germany.

Lead could pose the most serious threat to the boreal forests of the Northeast, because it accumulates faster than the other heavy trace metals. Measurements made in the early 1980s showed that lead concentrations in the forest soils of the Green Mountains in Vermont were within the range found in polluted urban mineral soils located near smelters and near heavily travelled highways. (See Figure 10.) On two occasions while scientists were collecting monthly precipitation samples in the White Mountains, the concentrations exceeded the public health standard for lead in drinking water.

Lead continues to accumulate in the forest despite conversion of automobiles to unleaded gasoline, because other sources contribute approximately 40 percent of the atmospheric lead. Nearly every bit of the lead that ends up in the forest stays there. Lead moves so slowly through northern forest soils that its mean retention time there can range from 500 to 5,000 years, depending on the types of soils involved. In some years, forty-four times more lead is added to the mountain soils of northern New England than leaves it. There is ten times more lead there now than there had been before the Industrial Revolution, and scientists estimate that, if current rates of accumulation continue, the amount of lead on the floors of these forests will double in twenty to thirty years.

Lead accumulates not only on the forest floor, but also on trees, mosses, and lichens. While studying lead accumulation in the White Mountains of New Hampshire, two scientists from the Yale School of Forestry and Environmental Studies, Siccama and William H. Smith, found substantial amounts of it on the needles, twigs, bark, and roots of red spruces and other plants. Some of the lead had even penetrated into the tissue of wood they obtained from the protected interior of red spruce stems. The roots contained about half of the lead associated with trees in the forest. Washing the roots until they appeared clean did not remove all of the lead. These scientists reported their findings in an article published by the *Journal of Environmental Quality* in the summer of 1981. "Lead concentration associated with the roots is high, but it has not been determined whether this is due to physiological uptake of Pb [lead] or contamination of the outer-root bark tissue."[5]

Since high-elevation forests receive substantially more precipitation than do lower elevations, forest soils at 4,000 feet contain approximately four times more lead than those at 1,300 feet. Vogelmann and Klein noted that the decline of red spruces also correlated with elevation—far more were dying at higher elevations than lower. They began to ask themselves whether the metals could be contributing to the decline of the trees. In 1978 an Austrian scientist, Dr. J. Greszta, reported that the accumulation of heavy metals in forest soil was damaging to spruce seedlings. Subsequently, Drs. D. L. Godbold and A. Hüttermann of the University of Göttingen, also discovered that the root growth of spruce seedlings was inhibited by lead, especially in nutrient-poor soil solutions.

Klein and Bliss performed a number of laboratory experiments designed to determine the effect of lead and other heavy metals on plants. They treated trees, mosses, bacteria, algae, and fungi with acidified water to which small amounts of aluminum, copper, lead or zinc had been added. The levels of acidity and metals they used were in the range of those found on Camels Hump. All the plants tested showed sharp growth declines, and many died. Cadmium, aluminum, and lead in acidic water each reduced the ability of spruce seedlings to take up water. Klein and Bliss were especially interested to see that a common moss they tested was most severely affected under the simulated field conditions. It is well known that mosses, which depend almost exclusively on the atmosphere for their nutrients, accumulate heavy metals, especially cadmium and lead. Since the mid-1960s, 47 percent of the mosses had disappeared from Camels Hump.

Klein noted another significant correlation. During the same period that the concentrations of heavy metals rapidly increased, the amount of litter on the forest floor also increased dramatically. Litter consists of all the dead needles, leaves, branches, cones, bark, and other organic matter that trees continually shed. A significant percentage of a forest's required nutrients is tied up in the litter, especially in the boreal zone where soils are the thinnest. Since litter decomposition is a slow process even under optimum conditions, any disruption of the process could have serious consequences for the forest's stability. Studies showed that from 1965 to 1982 the depth of the litter increased by 70 percent in the boreal forests on Camels Hump, signalling a substantial decrease in the rate of decomposition of the litter. Similar observations were reported by scientists in other remote, uncut and undeveloped virgin forests that appeared to be declining.

Fungi, bacteria, and other microbes play an important role in maintaining a healthy forest by helping to decompose the litter and recycle nutrients that trees need for continued growth. Klein wondered whether the presence of lead and other heavy metals in the acidic soil was interfering with the ability of the fungi and other organisms to decompose the litter. Copper, cadmium, nickel, lead, and zinc are all used to make fungicides, and studies in the White Mountains had shown that spruce litter had higher concentrations of lead than the litter of other major forest trees. Dr. Germund Tyler of the University of Lund, Sweden, demonstrated in 1973 that high levels of copper, lead, zinc, and other metals suppressed the ability of fungi to decompose and recycle spruce needle litter in the forest soils of central Sweden. Hutchinson and Whitby subsequently reported similar findings in the Sudbury region of Ontario. Klein believed that this might explain what was happening to the spruce litter on Camels Hump. Since a number of scientists in the United States still considered this theory to be unproven, Klein went back to the laboratory for more simulation experiments.

Klein and two students, Kirk A. Moloney and Lori A. Stratton, devised an experiment in which they exposed needle litter to water containing the same degree of acidity as in the boreal forest soils on Camels Hump: it repressed the metabolism of the microbes in the litter. When they added lead or zinc to the water in the range of concentrations found in the soil, the metabolism of the microbes was reduced further. Moloney, Stratton, and Klein published their findings in 1983 in the *Canadian Journal of Botany*:

. . .[T]he levels of insoluble metal complexes in soils and dissolved metal ions of Camels Hump mountainous ecosystems . . .are capable of reducing the metabolism of litter microflora, particularly when metal ions accompany acidic conditions. . . .Reductions in litter respiration could, over a 17-year period, account for the measured increase in litter depth with concomitant alterations in mineral cycling.[6]

That a theory proves to be true under controlled laboratory conditions does not necessarily mean that the theory is a fact in the wilderness. Nevertheless, if heavy metals in acidic soils could suppress the ability of fungi to decompose spruce litter in Sweden, in Canada, and in a laboratory in New England, there was no reason to believe that they could not also do it on Camels Hump. Yet, Klein decided upon another way to test the validity of the theory, this time in the field.

If it were true that the chemical makeup of the forest soil on Camels Hump was inhibiting the activity of fungi, then there should be fewer than normal mycorrhizae on the roots of the red spruces. Mycorrhizae are sensitive fungi that develop a symbiotic relationship with the young feeder roots of spruces and many other kinds of trees. Although scientists do not understand exactly how the fungi and trees benefit each other, they do know that destruction of the relationship alone is enough to weaken a tree. Scientists believe that mycorrhizae play a major role in enhancing a tree's ability to absorb nutrients and water, especially from poor soils. By covering the feeder roots with a coral-like mantle, mycorrhizae also protect the tree's roots from infection by harmful soil fungi.

Dr. Carl Olof Tamm, Professor of Forest Ecology at the College of Forestry in Stockholm and Chairman of the Swedish Committee of the International Biological Program, was one of the first scientists to consider the effects of acidity on mycorrhizae. In an article published in *Ambio* in 1976, he suggested that, since mycorrhizal roots are located largely in the top layer of the forest soil which is the layer first hit by acid rain, they could be very sensitive to acidification and should be seriously studied for possible long-term effects.[7] Virtually no work, however, had been done on this in the United States.

Klein had researchers take root samples from many small red spruces on Camels Hump, so that they could be examined for the tiny mycorrhizal growths. The scientists were consistently unable to find mycorrhizae on the roots of red spruces growing in the boreal zone. On the lower-elevation spruces they found that the mycorrhizae were not as abundant as they should be. Back in the laboratory, Klein subjected two kinds of fungi known to develop a mycorrhizal relationship with spruce, *Cenococcum graniforme* and *Polyporus circinatus*, to acidic water and heavy metals. He found that the growth of the fungi was repressed when he subjected them to a solution containing the same degree of acidity and the concentration ranges of copper, lead, and zinc found in the soils of Camels Hump.

In the summer of 1983, Vogelmann and Bliss, along with Helen Whitney, a graduate student at the University of Vermont, resurveyed the stands on Camels Hump surveyed by Siccama in the mid-1960s and again in 1979. They wanted to determine whether there had been further changes in the condition of the forests. As Vogelmann suspected, the decline had not only continued since 1979, but it had intensified. The amount (volume by weight) of living wood had continued to decline substantially in all three forest zones on the mountain—by 19 percent in the lower hardwood zone; by 11 percent in the transition zone; and by 41 percent in the high-elevation boreal zone. Nearly every species of tree on Camels

Hump had participated in the continuing general decline, even the two species (yellow birch and white birch) that had shown growth up to 1979.

Again, the boreal forest was the most severely affected. From 1965 to 1983 the amount of living red spruce wood declined 71 percent. Balsam fir, its principal competitor, declined by 19 percent. White birch, the only tree in the boreal forest that had shown continued growth up to 1979, was devastated; since 1979 the volume of its wood had declined by 43 percent.

The picture in the lower-elevation forests was not much better. Sugar maple, which had declined by 16 percent from 1965 to 1979, was down by 25 percent four years later. Mountain ash had declined by 39 percent since 1965; and mountain maple by 61 percent. The only tree that had shown growth in the hardwood forest up to 1979 was now declining too; from 1979 to 1983, yellow birch had dropped 10 percent. Striped maple was at about the same level in 1983 as it had been in 1979, but down 23 percent overall since 1965. Only one tree, American beech, had been able to respond to the competitive opportunity offered by its declining neighbors: American beech had increased its volume by 7 percent from 1979 to 1983; yet, its small gain could not begin to offset the enormous losses of the other trees.

As distressing as these findings were, the inability to find young trees was an even more serious concern. A population of trees can be decimated, but as long as it can propagate, there is hope for the future. Without the ability to reproduce, the species sooner or later will disappear from the area. One of the best ways to measure the ability of a tree to reproduce is to count the number of its seedlings and saplings in the forest. Vogelmann, Whitney, Bliss, and several other botany students combed through the forests at all elevations on Camels Hump looking for young trees. They

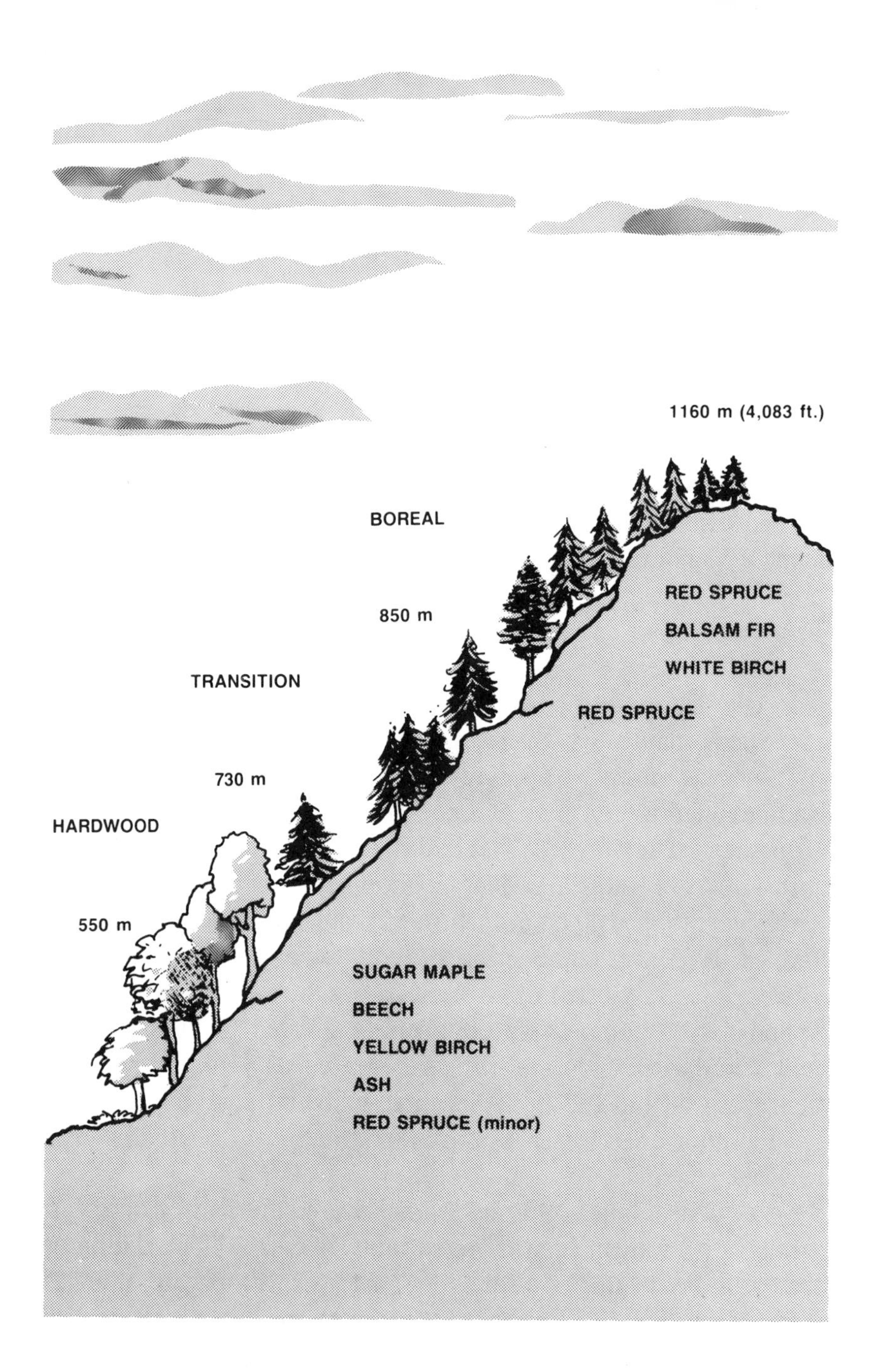

Fig. 11 — Distribution of Tree Species on Camels Hump, Vermont.

Source: Environmental Protection Agency, 1987.

discovered that from 1965 to 1983 the number of red spruce saplings and seedlings in the forests declined by 80 percent; the decline in the last four years alone was 65 percent. The other members of the boreal community were having the same problem. The number of small balsam firs, for example, had dropped by 54 percent from 1979 to 1983; and white birches had dropped in number by 77 percent. In the lower-elevation forests, the same loss of reproduction appeared. Since 1965 the density of sugar maple seedlings and saplings declined by 84 percent; American beech by 64 percent; mountain maple by 39 percent. Two trees that had been reproducing well up to 1979 reversed the trend thereafter—from 1979 to 1983 the rate of yellow birch reproduction declined by 56 percent; and mountain ash by 7 percent. Only the striped maple, whose small overall population made it a relatively unimportant member of the forest, was able to show increased reproduction.

Since there are many factors affecting the ability of a seed to develop into a tree, the Acidic Deposition Research Project would have to look at each of them. First, the parent tree must be able to produce cones and viable seeds. Even a healthy tree will not produce an abundant crop of seeds every year, but the number of viable cones and seeds may decrease when the tree is under stress. In the autumn, red spruce cones ripen and begin to open, releasing their seeds—about 175,000 seeds per bushel of cones. As the seeds pour out of the cones from October to March, the winds disseminate them throughout the forest up to 200 feet from the parent tree. Everything depends on where the seeds land. If they end up on sod, rock, or standing water, they are doomed. Most of them land on the litter that covers most of the forest floor, which may or may not be hospitable. Litter is one of the weapons a tree uses to protect its territory from invasion by competing trees. Red spruce litter, for example, contains organic substances produced by the tree that effectively prevent the seeds of other trees from germinating in it. The other trees, of course, do the same in return, which explains why yellow birches do not mix with red spruce.

In order for a seed to become established as a seedling, it must get under the litter and then under the duff (partly decomposed litter) so that its main root can penetrate into the humus-mineral layer of the soil. The seed has a little less than a year to do this before it either rots, loses its viability, or is eaten by a rodent or a bird. In order to germinate, the seed needs adequate moisture, temperature, and shade. A red spruce seed appreciates shade; too much direct sunlight can repress germination. If the parent trees are defoliated or blown down, the protective shading is lost.

As hard as it is for a red spruce seed to germinate, it is even more difficult for a red spruce seedling to survive to become a sapling. Most red spruce seeds germinate in the forest during the early spring, just as the excessively acidic and contaminated meltwater is coursing through the soils. Spruce seedlings have unusually shallow, slow-growing root systems. A two-year-old red spruce seedling is likely to be less than 2.5 cm tall with roots less than 5 cm deep. Therefore, their rate of survival depends greatly upon the quantity and quality of the mineral soil and the water. Finally, red spruce seedlings are so tiny and grow so slowly that they can be smothered or crushed by the litter that falls most heavily in the autumn and by the frequent winter frost-heaving of soils.

Despite these obstacles, red spruces reproduced and thrived for hundreds of thousands of years in the severest of climates. Vogelmann and Klein wanted to know why the forests on Camels Hump and elsewhere had stopped producing seedlings and saplings. The laboratory experiments conducted by Klein and Bliss demonstrated convincingly that simulated acidic precipitation and toxic metals could damage roots and kill red spruce seedlings;

still, the problem of declining reproduction warranted further investigation.

Although most of the mature red spruce trees had died, the survivors seemed to be producing some viable seeds. An examination of their cones showed seeds that appeared normal and viable. Perhaps something prevented the viable seeds from germinating after they reached the ground. Klein wondered whether the excess acids and toxic metals in the precipitation and soils could be repressing the germination of forest tree seeds. Dr. G. Abrahamsen in Norway had found in 1975 that pH values below 4.0 retarded the germination of Norway spruce seeds. Scherbatskoy and Klein decided to test the idea with red spruce, balsam fir, yellow birch, and paper birch seeds in the laboratory. The results were not conclusive. Neither acids nor metals seemed to have a consistent effect on germination of the seeds. If anything, high acidity seemed to help stimulate the germination of balsam fir and yellow birch seeds, perhaps by weakening the seed coat. They concluded that it was unlikely that acids or metals directly caused any reduced germination of seeds in the forests.

It was possible, however, that air pollution could be having an indirect effect on seed germination in the forest by slowing down the ability of fungi and other microbes to decompose the litter. A number of scientists, such as Dr. B. Moore of the United States, Dr. I. C. Place of Canada, and Dr. M. V. Kolesnichenko of the Soviet Union, had suggested earlier that changes in the depth of forest floor litter could affect the germination of spruce seeds by changing the temperature, moisture balance, and concentration of repressive substances in the soils.

Scherbatskoy and Klein designed another experiment to test whether changes in litter depth affected the germination of tree seeds. In the laboratory, they sowed a variety of seeds on different combinations of soil, duff, and litter. The soil they used was regular greenhouse potting soil; the litter comprised of red spruce and balsam fir needles gathered from healthy trees on Camels Hump; the duff came from the boreal zone on the mountain. They discovered that seeds of red spruce, balsam fir, paper birch, and yellow birch all germinated well when they were sown on clear potting soil or on soil covered to small depths of litter or duff. But when the depth of litter exceeded two centimeters, none of the seeds would germinate. Red spruce seeds were more sensitive to litter depth than the others; they would not germinate on more than one centimeter of the litter or duff. A chemical analysis of the litter indicated that it contained organic compounds that inhibited germination of the seeds. Wetting the litter or duff with water having a pH of 4.1 did not remove the substances that were repressing the germination of red spruce seeds. Therefore, Scherbatskoy and Klein concluded that the increased depths of litter in the forests could be responsible for preventing red spruce seeds from germinating because of the increased amounts of repressive substances in the litter.

By September of 1983, Vogelmann and Klein were satisfied that their field and laboratory work had produced more than enough evidence to prove that air pollution was probably causing the profound decline of great forests in Vermont and the rest of the northern Appalachian mountains. Yet, no one pollutant was solely to blame. Rather, they believed that the cumulative effect of all identified pollutants working together had triggered the decline.

By filling the air with poisonous gases and repeatedly drenching the trees with acidic precipitation, air pollution was damaging the foliage, stripping it of essential nutrients and products, and reducing the amounts of nutrients that were available to the trees in the soils by stripping them away at an accelerated rate with sulfuric and nitric acids. Polluted air was also poisoning the water supply of the trees by filling the soil solution with toxic concentrations of aluminum, lead, and other metallic chemicals that kill roots and reduce their ability to absorb the water and nutrients they need. By turning the soils into a sink of toxic acids and chemicals, air pollution was killing the helpful fungi that usually form the beneficial mycorrhizal association with tree roots. The polluted air was also repressing the ability of other helpful fungi and microbes to decompose the forest litter, the only process by which the diminished stores of essential nutrients could be replenished. At the same time, the changes in the chemistry and depth of the forest-floor litter was apparently suppressing the ability of tree seeds to germinate and become viable saplings.

In a paper presented at the George Aiken Memorial Technical Symposium on acid rain held in Burlington, Vermont, on September 22, 1983, Klein and Vogelmann told the assembled scientists:

There is now no question that damage represents a ''clear and present danger,'' and that some damage may be effectively permanent.... Put simply, the Camels Hump ecosystems in Vermont is a catastrophe in progress, and both our field and our laboratory studies are fully and solely compatible with the working hypothesis that the declines are due largely to the combined actions of acids and solubilized metals.[8]

The conclusion that air pollution was killing the forests was consistent with the facts and explained the evidence found in the laboratory and on the mountains. It explained why the once abundant red spruce trees that used to live for more than 300 years were now dying prematurely; why red spruces of every age covering an enormous geographical area were dying simultaneously in the Northeast; why other, very different types of trees like sugar maples and balsam firs were also declining; why trees in the Northeast were affected but not trees of the same kind located in less polluted environments; why trees growing on different types of soils and subject to very different climatic conditions were nevertheless all dying in Europe and North America; why evergreen trees were more severely hit than broadleaf trees; why trees at higher elevations were dying in larger numbers than lower-elevation forest trees; why trees on the westward sides of mountains were more severely damaged than trees on the easterly sides.

The case against air pollution was consistent with the fact that healthy forests suddenly began to decline in the 1950s in the Northeast; that the amounts of aluminum and vanadium had increased dramatically in the wood of the red spruce trees since the early 1950s; that the roots of the red spruce trees were discolored and unhealthy; that there were abnormally low levels of calcium in the roots of declining red spruces on Camels Hump; that the trees look like they are suffering from drought even though there are adequate amounts of moisture in the soils; that the trees are losing their needles and leaves from the top down and the outside in; that the balsam firs are not taking over the growing spaces defaulted by the dead red spruces.

The conclusion that air pollution was to blame could explain why there was little or no mycorrhizal development on the roots of red spruces; why half the mosses had disappeared from Camels Hump; why the amount of undecomposed litter on the forest floors had nearly doubled; why there was an elevated amount of sulfur in the foliage of the red spruce trees; why the forests began to decline long before any drought and continued to decline long after the droughts of the mid-1960s had ceased; and why there were so few precious seedlings and saplings in the forest.

Vogelmann and Klein had accepted the risks of devoting a large part of their careers to the pursuit of a difficult and controversial theory. They had pursued the evidence to its most probable conclusion, and they were putting their professional reputations on the line in the scientific community by announcing that, in their opinion, without air pollution, the trees would probably not be failing. They sat back and awaited the verdict of their peers and hoped that their work would not be ignored as the earlier contributions of Robert Angus Smith and Eville Gorham had been. Vogelmann was especially interested to see what Tom Siccama would say.

Where Does Acid Rain Fall?

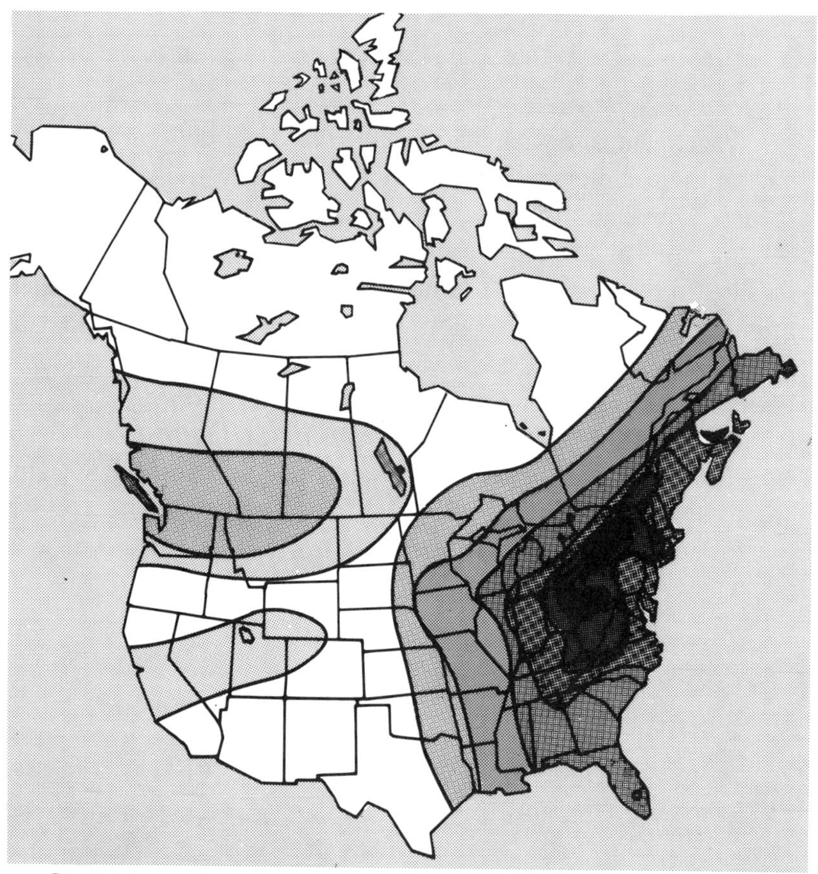

CURRENT ANNUAL SULFATE DEPOSITION LEVELS

- 5-10 kg./ha.
- 10-15 kg.½/ha.
- 15-20 kg./ha.
- 20-25 kg./ha.
- 25-30 kg./ha.
- 30-40 kg./ha.
- 40 + kg./ha.

Fig. 12 — Annual Sulfate Deposition Levels.

The map depicts acid rain in North America, measured in kilograms per hectare according to international measuring standards. Levels exceeding 20kg./ha. (18 lb./acre) per year are regarded as threatening to moderately sensitive aquatic and terrestrial ecosystems. Source: *Fact Sheet on Acid Rain*. Prepared for the Canadian Embassy by Wellford, Weyman, Krulwich, Gold and Huff, 1984.

5

The Search for Natural Causes

Siccama was considered by many to be an authority on the ecology of the forests in the northern Appalachian Mountains. With the possible exception of Vogelmann, probably no other scientist in the United States had spent more time studying the Green Mountain forests. He also had a reputation among scientists as a blunt and demanding critic. His view of the accumulating scientific evidence would be taken seriously by others.

Siccama followed the progress of the scientists at the University of Vermont and elsewhere, and he performed a substantial amount of field work of his own. He knew that the red spruces in the high-elevation forests of northern New England and New York were suffering widespread mortality and decline and that other species such as balsam fir and white birch were also losing ground in many locations. He agreed that the mountain summits in the Northeast were being subjected to extraordinarily high amounts of air pollution and acid precipitation, as were the highlands of West Germany, where large tracts of Norway spruce and silver fir also showed similar symptoms. Nevertheless, Siccama did not agree that the case against air pollution had been proven. In his opinion, the evidence was still insufficient to justify his former teacher's conclusion that air pollution was probably responsible for the declining forests.

Siccama elaborated on his objections in a series of papers he and a soil scientist, Dr. Arthur H. Johnson of the University of Pennsylvania, published in *Environmental Science & Technology*[1] and the *Tappi Journal*[2]. They did not dispute the claim that air pollution could be the principal cause of the red spruce devastation. The laboratory work of Klein and others persuaded Siccama and Johnson that there were several logical pathways by which air pollution could be stressing the forests and causing the observed symptoms of mortality and decline.

> Because of the documented accumulation of heavy metals, the high rates of acidic deposition, the prolonged contact with acid mist, and laboratory evidence that reasonable levels of dissolved aluminum and possibly other metals can alter water movement in red spruce, anthropogenic pollutants may be involved in the red spruce decline.[3]

They also acknowledged that at least one of the by-products of air pollution, acid precipitation, was in fact stressing forests. Their doubts about the air pollution theory were based upon a subtle analysis of the concept of "causation."

Forest ecosystems are so complex that there is rarely a single cause for an effect. This holds especially true for forests subject to environmental stress. Since insects and diseases had been ruled out as the primary causes of the decline, Siccama and Johnson believed that the problem of the red spruce was essentially environmental. "Given the lack of other causal agents and the characteristics of the observed dieback, it appears that the mortality is probably related to some environmental stress or combination of stresses."[4] In cases like this there were three kinds of causes to look for. First, there may have been one or more "predisposing causes", stresses that weakened the trees or somehow made them susceptible to injuries they might not otherwise have suffered. Changing climate, poor site conditions, and exposure to long-term air pollution were examples of the kinds of environmental stresses that Siccama and Johnson believed could have predisposed the red spruces to the decline and mortality. Second, there may have been one or more "precipitating causes"—

drought, frost damage, or an episode of severe air pollution damage—which actually triggered the widespread decline of the trees. Third, there may have been one or more "contributing causes", such as a subsequent invasion by insects or infection by fungi, which have added to the overall stress on the forests.

Siccama and Johnson agreed that acid precipitation and fallout did in fact stress the forests in the Northeast. They questioned, however, the importance of that stress in the context of all the other possible stresses. In their judgment, the evidence was not clear enough to establish that the stress from the acids and other forms of air pollution was anything more than a minor contributing cause to the decline.

One of the reasons for their reservation was that the air pollution theory did not explain all the data they had seen. For example, when they measured the aluminum content of 120 trees, they found no consistent differences between the healthy and declining stands. They also found that the ratio of calcium to aluminum in the foliage and the roots of the trees increased with increasing elevation. Since the theory proposed that acid precipitation released toxic levels of soluble aluminum that harmed the trees, one might expect the declining trees to contain more aluminum than the healthy trees and the high-elevation trees to contain lower calcium to aluminum ratios than low-elevation trees. Therefore, this aspect of the theory seemed to be inconsistent with these findings from 120 trees, and it gave Siccama and Johnson a reason to question the theory. "We reserve final judgment on the Al (aluminum) question . . . until additional information is available."[5]

Siccama and Johnson also disagreed with some of the scientific methods Vogelmann and Klein employed in their work. For example, Siccama and Johnson disputed the values used by Klein, Moloney, and Stratton to determine the extent and cause of increased litter depth on Camels Hump.

The principal reason why Siccama and Johnson were not convinced that the case against air pollution had been proved, however, was because other possible causes of the decline had not yet been fully ruled out. They wrote:

> Acid deposition is but one of many stress factors acting on forests. As research progresses, it will be necessary to give equal treatment to several potential factors about which we currently have little quantitative information, such as . . .long-term climate change . . . and the effects of drought.[6]

As long as a plausible case could still be made for the proposition that the decline of trees was due to a natural environmental cause (such as natural-stand dynamics, long-term climatic changes, poor site conditions, drought or winter damage), then the case against man-made air pollution would remain unproved in the minds of Siccama and Johnson.

In their search for environmental forces that could have predisposed the red spruces to suffer their decline, one of the first subjects that Siccama and Johnson explored was site conditions. Adverse site conditions are important environmental factors that can predispose trees to injury and decline. Trees growing in a harsh climate or on nutrient-poor soils, for example, will be less able to withstand added stress than trees of the same species growing on more favorable sites.

Wind is a natural condition that can adversely affect the quality of a forest site. High-elevation spruce-fir forests in the northern Appalachian Mountains are among the windiest in the world. In most regions of the world, temperature is considered to be the most important environmental determinant of the tree line. In the northern Appalachians, however, the primary determinant of tree line is the wind. This is true of only two other places of the world—northern Japan and Scotland. As long as there is no change in wind exposure, these high-elevation forests are able to cope with this natural force. If, however, a swath is cut through the forest to install a road, ski trail, or power line, or if the canopy of the forest is opened by severe logging or by the windthrow or death of dominant trees, then trees on the downwind edge of the gap suffer wind damage. Many of the symptoms of wind damage are similar to the symptoms of the declining and dying red spruces throughout the East. Thus, although wind damage could explain only a portion of the observed mortality, it was a factor to consider.

Siccama and Johnson performed a correlation analysis in which they tried to relate the decline of the red spruce to a number of environmental parameters. The only parameter that correlated significantly with the mortality of red spruce was elevation; that is, there was a very clear increase in mortality with increasing elevation. They also found that several environmental stress factors in the Northeast were related to elevation. Wind speed, exposure to cloud and fog moisture, acid precipitation, and the heavy-metal content of the soils all increased with elevation. Other factors such as soil and air temperature, capacity of the soils to hold moisture, soil pH, and the availability of basic minerals like potassium, calcium, magnesium, and manganese all decreased with increasing elevation. Several factors (wind speed and temperature, for example) had been natural to the region since the beginning of time, while others (like acid precipitation and heavy metals) resulted from recent man-made air pollution. All stressed the trees to some extent and probably predisposed them to decline.

Siccama and Johnson concluded that two sets of forces could plausibly have predisposed the red spruces to harm. The adverse site conditions caused by man-made air pollution could have weakened the trees and made them susceptible to mortal injury. But it was also plausible that the severe environmental conditions that naturally exist on the mountains alone could have left the high-elevation red spruces vulnerable to setback. As long as both sets of forces were probably involved, it would be impossible to say whether the air pollution stresses represented a large or small part of the picture. Johnson summed up this conclusion:

> Thus if the indirect effects of acid deposition acting on soil properties are important predisposing stresses, it will probably not be possible to identify them as such, since so many other stresses increase in severity with increasing altitude.[7]

Their inquiry, of course, could not end there. Naturally severe site conditions could have predisposed the red spruces to injury, yet, the trees had been successfully coping with those conditions for millennia. Something else had come along in the 1950s or 1960s to trigger a decline from which the trees never recovered. The advent of unnaturally acidic precipitation and worsening air pollution during that period could have precipitated the decline. The question was whether Siccama and Johnson could find any other natural forces that could also have triggered the mortality.

There are more than thirty different species of spruce trees in the world, and geneticists believe that they all developed from a single ancestral type originating in northern Asia. Over the course of many thousands of years, spruces migrated from Asia eastward across boreal routes into Canada, and then moved southward along mountain chains into the United States and Mexico. In the process, they evolved into the eight different species of spruces that are now native to North America.

Two prehistoric events made it possible for spruce to migrate down the Appalachian Mountains into North Carolina and Tennessee—the evolution of the red spruce as a distinct species (the only species of spruce able to compete successfully with the wide variety of vegetation found throughout the Appalachians) and a series of long-term climatic changes that offered the red spruce the opportunity to find in the highest elevations of the southern mountains approximately the same temperature and moisture conditions as it enjoyed in the northern end of its habitat. (See Figure 13.) Natural powers that create opportunities, however, can also take them away. The same evolutionary and climatic forces that created the conditions which enabled the original stand of red spruces to succeed in the Appalachians could also have changed conditions over time in a way that predisposed the current stand to widespread failure. Siccama and Johnson asked whether there was anything about the nature of the red spruce or its climate that was making the trees vulnerable to a wide-scale decline. One of the first areas they investigated was the red spruce's inherited growth habits.

Since forest trees must continually compete with each other for essential nutrients and sunlight, scientists expect to see a certain amount of mortality among trees even in a healthy, growing forest. The natural dynamics of forest competition can cause large shifts to occur in some tree populations over several centuries. The life cycle of the balsam fir is a notable example. Balsam firs are genetically programmed to grow in relatively pure, dense stands of even-aged trees. While fir seedlings and saplings mature together, large numbers die, and the stand naturally thins itself, leaving

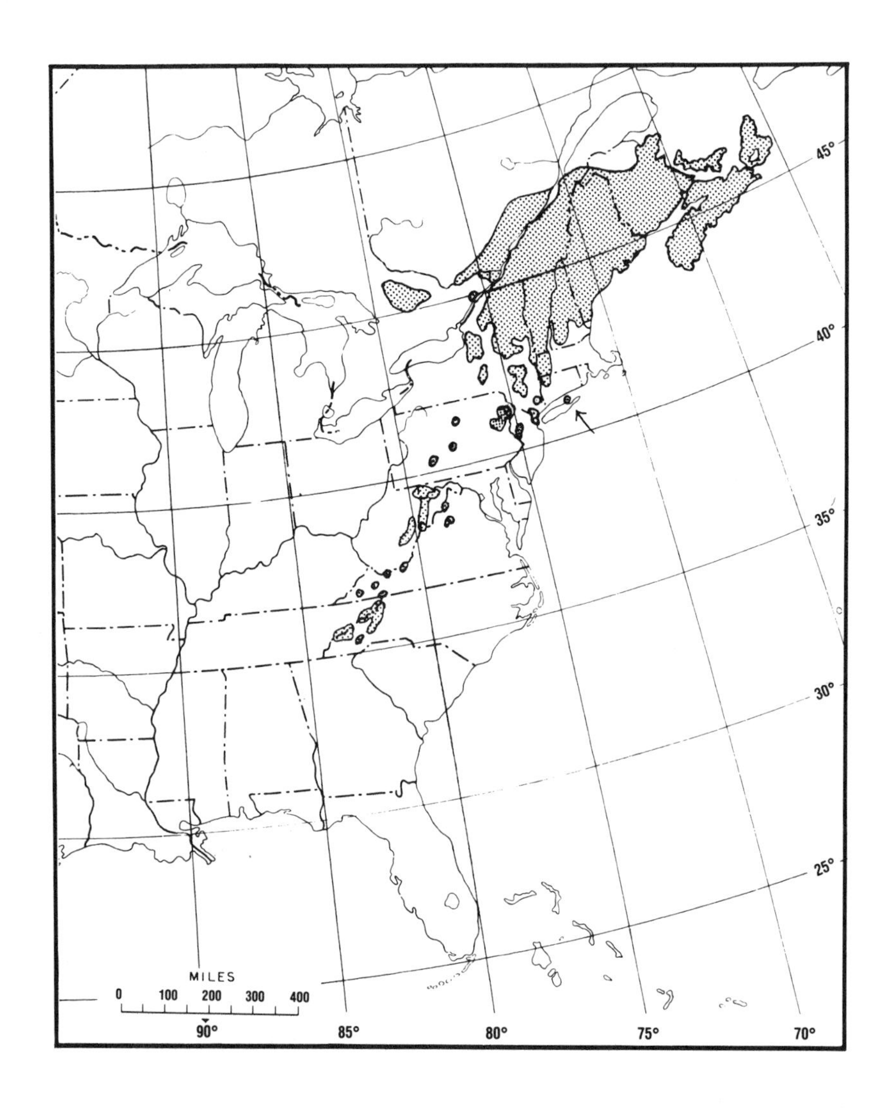

Fig. 13 — Natural Range of Red Spruce in North America.

Source: USDA Forest Service, 1986.

only the strongest to mature. A century or so later, after the balsams have grown old, the stand will suddenly collapse from the synchronized death of the ancient firs. This natural cycle of death and regeneration has been known to result in the sudden death of up to one-third of the balsam firs in some locations. When the firs disappear, their space becomes available for colonization by competing tree species.

Unlike the balsam firs, red spruces have not been genetically preconditioned to experience cycles of synchronized mortality. Old-growth and virgin stands containing a mixture of young, middle-aged and old red spruces ordinarily sustain growth for several centuries. There is evidence, however, that even-aged stands of red spruce, stands in which most of the trees are of approximately the same age, may behave quite differently. Stands of this type can result from heavy logging and other disturbances like fire, farming, and insect infestation. After the loggers have left and the disturbance has abated, a generation of even-aged spruces may begin to take over the site. Many years later, they reach maturity at approximately the same time. The number of years it takes for them to reach maturity depends on the biological-carrying capacity of the site on which they are growing. For many sites in the Northeast, that point could be reached after only fifty or sixty years. After that, the growth rate of the even-aged stand of red spruce will flatten out and then enter into a period of decline that could last for many years.

The eastern United States saw a great deal of logging around the turn of the century. As a consequence, many red spruces in the East are growing in even-aged stands made up of trees that either germinated between 1900 and 1910, or germinated earlier but were suppressed until their competitors, the larger and older trees, were removed by loggers in the early 1900s. Some of these stands are probably growing on poor-quality sites with a limited biological-carrying capacity. Those stands could have reached their maturity in the early 1960s and then begun to decline from natural competitive interaction, even in the absence of air pollution. Thus, the concept of natural stand dynamics or "the law of self-thinning", as it is sometimes called, is probably responsible for part of the decline of the red spruce that began in the early 1960s in the Northeast. The question for Siccama and Johnson was whether these natural competitive forces were likely to have been a substantial factor in the overall decline of the red spruce.

Natural stand dynamics could explain why some red spruces declined on some sites, but the decline of the red spruce was regionwide and encompassed not only even-aged stands but also old-growth, virgin forests. Trees on all types of sites, good and bad, declined, and so did young red spruces well under the age of fifty years and far from reaching their maturity. Siccama and Johnson concluded that natural stand dynamics could not explain the widespread decline of the trees: "Since spruce mortality in the U.S. occurred in both regenerating and virgin stands in all size classes, and since the mortality and dieback are so extensive, it is unlikely that a combination of natural thinning and breakup of old stands accounts for the observed mortality."[8]

Although the normal life cycle of the red spruce did not predispose it to such a large-scale decline, perhaps a climatic change did. A significant change in such climatic factors as mean annual temperature, cloud cover, and rainfall can affect the growth and abundance of various forest tree species. The composition of forests can also change in response to long-term changes in climate, although scientists cannot yet predict with accuracy the magnitude or duration of a forest's response. The relationship between vegetation and climate is so well recognized, however, that scientists sometimes use the fossil remains of vegetation to deduce historical and prehistorical changes in the earth's climate. These deductions are based upon the traditional assumptions that plants respond immediately to changes in climate and that the distribution and abundance of vegetation are always in equilibrium with the climate of the location where they live.

No substantial climatic changes have occurred within the past few decades that could account for the decline of the red spruce and other trees in the Northeast. Climatologists believe that the average temperature of the globe peaked in the 1940s, that it fell until 1970, and then began rising again. However, the temperature changes involved were very small; from the 1940s to about 1970, there was only a 0.3° to 0.4° C decline in mean annual temperature in the Northern Hemisphere, not enough to seriously affect the health and composition of the forests.

Recent studies, however, have called into question the traditional assumptions about how plants respond to changes in climate. In 1983, Dr. Margaret Bryan Davis of the University of Minnesota and Dr. Daniel B. Botkin of the University of California tested these assumptions with the aid of computer models designed to simulate the growth of the cool-temperature forests of northern New England. They programmed the computer to simulate a variety of abrupt temperature changes of up to 2° C to see how the forest models would respond. They found that the forest models did indeed respond to the changes in temperature, but not immediately. Forest responses lagged chronologically behind temperature changes, sometimes by as many as 100 to 150 years under certain site conditions. Moreover, because of the delayed responses, the distribution and abundance of the various species of trees were not always in equilibrium with the climate. They theorized that the delayed responses occurred because the tree species (sugar maple, red spruce, and others) were long-lived and had an innate ability to tolerate a wide range of climatic conditions.

Davis and Botkin reported their findings in *Quaternary Research:*

Mature trees have a high average survival rate even under climatic stress. Furthermore, a closed, mature tree canopy strongly influences light conditions near the forest floor, and therefore strongly influences regeneration. . . . Our results agree with Smith's (1965) idea of community "inertia" in response to climatic change. He suggested a similar mechanism: When climatic change occurs, adult perennial plants continue to survive, but do not reproduce successfully. Young plants of other species, better adapted to the new climatic regime, enter the community gradually, and existing plants are replaced as they die by invading species.[9]

Studies such as this suggested that temperature changes that occurred 100 to 150 years ago could have predetermined changes in forest composition occurring today. The Northern Hemisphere underwent what is called "the Little Ice Age," a period lasting several centuries and ending about 1850, during which mean annual temperatures fell about 2°C. From about 1850 until the late 1940s, mean annual temperature in the Northern Hemisphere rose 0.6°C. Could the forest declines that began in the 1950s or 1960s be a 100-year delayed response to temperatures that began rising around 1850? Siccama and Johnson concluded that climatic changes were probably not involved in the red spruce decline.

A number of facts supported this conclusion. For example, the changes in temperature did not occur abruptly, but gradually. This suggested that the delayed response predicted by the computer simulations would not be apparent so soon after the trend in temperature reversed around 1850. Also, one might expect red spruce reproduction to be affected by a warming trend, but one would not expect adult red spruce trees to be dying as the result of so small a change in degree. If forests in the Northeast today were already responding to a warming trend that began about 100 years ago, one would expect to see a shift in the relative growth rate of red spruces at some point along the elevational gradient of the mountains. Trees at one elevation would be benefitted at the expense of trees at another. In other words, red spruces would be seen growing at higher or lower elevations than they ever had before. This would be expected even in the northern Appalachians where tree line is primarily determined by wind velocity; it is also affected by temperature, although to a smaller extent. None of these happened in the Northeast—instead, red spruces at all elevations were in a state of decline, and no other species of trees appeared to be taking their places. As a final measure, Siccama, Johnson, and other scientists took numerous tree cores whose rings of growth dated back more than 200 years. The rings showed large variations in annual growth, but they did not consistently correlate with any climatic changes.

For several years Siccama, Johnson, and others claimed that the decline of the red spruce may have been triggered by a drought. The word "drought" has a variety of different meanings. The U.S. Weather Bureau considers a drought to be a period of three weeks or longer when the rainfall averages only 30 percent for the time and place. The widely used Palmer Drought Index, which is also based on the amount of precipitation in an area, measures cumulative moisture conditions on a scale from 0 (normal) to -5 (very extreme drought). The botanist considers inadequate any definition of drought that is based solely upon precipitation, because many other factors (such as slope, elevation, ground water, plant cover, and cloud water interception) also affect drought. To the botanist, a plant will not suffer drought damage unless its soil contains little or no available water.

By almost any standard, the drought which struck the New England and mid-Atlantic states during the early to mid-1960s was a serious one. The Palmer Drought Index for Vermont showed that the summers from 1962 to 1966 were more frequently and intensely dry than any other period since 1895. In the summer of 1962 the Index read -5; only once before, in the summer of 1941, had it ever dipped below -3 in Vermont. (See Figure 14.)

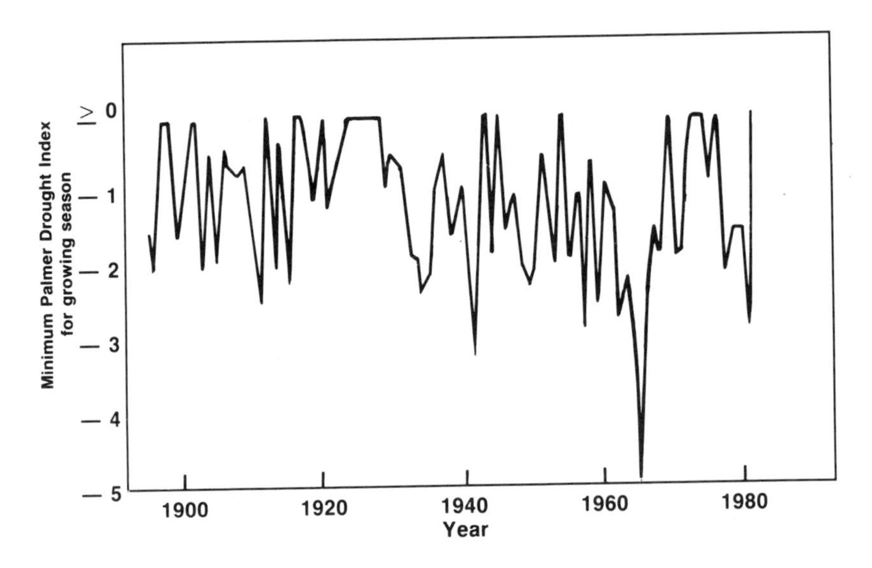

Fig. 14 — Palmer Drought Index for Vermont, 1895-1981*.

*This is based on average weather data. The minimum value for the growing season (May-August) is shown in this index. O represents an average year, and negative numbers indicate that precipitation is less than normal. Source: T.J. Blasing, Oak Ridge National Laboratory, Oak Ridge, Tenn. Reprinted with permission from *Environmental Science & Technology,* 1983, 17, 299. Copyright 1982 American Chemical Society.

Water is of prime importance for tree development. Up to 95 percent of the fresh weight of a tree's green tissues is water. Water transports essential substances to and from the tree's living cells and is a component in the tree's production of carbohydrates and other vital compounds. The water in a tree also helps to keep a tree cool during hot summer days when the temperature of the bark on its south side may reach 130° F and when soil temperatures approach 170° F. Without adequate water a tree begins to dehydrate and overheat, and if these conditions continue, they alter the tree's normal metabolism. The foliage of an evergreen tree suffering from moisture stress first wilts, then turns yellow and brown, and finally dies. A series of hot, dry growing seasons interferes with the normal growth of fine roots, especially in seedlings, and a protracted drought frequently triggers a gradual decline in the vigor of many tree species. An especially severe drought can kill the foliage, twigs, and branches at the crown of the trees. Since these were the general symptoms displayed by the declining red spruces, Siccama and Johnson suspected that the drought of the early to mid-1960s had precipitated the forest decline in the Northeast.

Siccama and Johnson took increment cores from 700 red spruces in both the northern and southern Appalachian Mountains. The tree ring records confirmed that the majority of the trees in the Northeast had experienced an abrupt and widespread shift to substantially smaller annual growth rings in the early to mid-1960s, the period of the drought. However, the rings also showed that in all northern stands sampled, the growth rate of trees had begun to decline long before the arrival of the drought. The first abnormal growth rings appeared in different years from site to site and in different years even among trees at the same site, but in all cases a decreasing growth trend was already evident before the drought had reached even moderate severity (-2 on the Palmer Drought Index). Apparently something else triggered a decline of the trees, a decline which was then dramatically accelerated by the drought.

The tree rings revealed another trend that tended to undermine the theory that drought had precipitated the decline. At all northern sites, the growth rates of red spruces continued to decline long after the drought ended. If the onset of drought stress had triggered the decline, then the drought's end should have arrested the decline. Instead, however, the decline not only continued but intensified over time. Droughts are a normal part of long-term weather cycles, occurring fairly regularly. These northern stands of red spruce trees growing under adverse conditions had recovered from many severe droughts over the past three or four centuries. The fact that they had not recovered from this last one disturbed Siccama and Johnson: "The prolonged nature of the diminished growth is . . . difficult to account for. It suggests permanent alterations in physiology or, perhaps, continuing stress."[10]

The results of their tree ring studies gave Siccama and Johnson reason to doubt the theory that drought had precipitated the red spruce decline. When Siccama reviewed unpublished data he and others had collected 20 years previously on Camels Hump and Hubbard Brook, he also had reason to doubt that there had even been a drought in the high-elevation spruce-fir forests of the Northeast. The botanist's definition of drought emphasizes the amount of moisture there is in the soil; if there is adequate soil moisture, then the plants do not suffer drought injury even though precipitation rates may be low.

There are many factors that affect the levels of soil moisture in the high-elevation Appalachians besides precipitation. The spruce-fir forests of the Northeast have a countless number of small twigs and needles that collectively add up to an enormous surface area—nearly 14 million yards per acre. By efficiently trapping water droplets from the frequent clouds and fogs that immerse the mountain peaks, these needles and twigs add three inches of moisture to the soil for every four inches that fall as precipitation each year in the subalpine zone. The same heavy coat of evergreen needles also retards evaporation of the moisture from the forest soil.

In the summers of 1965, 1966, and 1967, during the peak of the drought in the Northeast, Siccama conducted an extensive sampling of the moisture on the forest floor on Camels Hump. His unpublished field notes showed that the amount of available surface water during those summers always exceeded the capacity of the soil to absorb it all. Soil moisture had not been limited on Camels Hump. Another study conducted by Siccama at Hubbard Brook during that same period of drought suggested that the trees there grew better during dry years than they did in wet years. The journal article Siccama co-authored with Vogelmann and Bliss in 1982 stated: "Spruce was the species most predictively responsive to these variables thus indicating that in these soils, dry conditions favor growth rather than retard it. The symptoms of drought stress in spruce may not be related to the amount of water available in the soil, but rather to the trees' ability to take up that water."[11]

By January of 1985, Siccama was prepared to declare: "Drought is not a very likely prospect. It doesn't hang together as a plausible theory."[12] The most that could fairly be said about the drought of the early to mid-1960s was that for several years it contributed to a decline that had been set in motion by some other force.

Because of its longevity and its growth patterns in response to temperature fluctuations, red spruce is often used by scientists to help reconstruct historical and prehistorical climatic conditions. A number of scientists studying long-term chronologies of red spruce tree rings have noted an unusual pattern. When unusually high temperatures in late summer (July and August) are followed by unusually cold temperatures in early winter (December and

January), the growth of the tree the following spring is often below normal. There are no generally accepted explanations why this should be so.

Johnson and two of his colleagues from the University of Pennsylvania, Dr. Andrew J. Friedland and Jonathan D. Dushoff, decided to look into unusual temperature fluctuations at the time of the decline of the red spruce. They gathered information from long-term temperature records kept at various locations in upper New York State and in Burlington, Vermont, identifying each of the occasions when above-average temperatures in August were followed by below-average temperatures in December. They found several such episodes since 1820, the earliest year for which they had collected temperature data. One of these episodes, which occurred in the late 1950s, roughly correlated with the onset of the red spruce decline. It was followed by another like episode in the late 1960s, and still another in the mid-1970s.

Johnson and the others reviewed historical accounts of forest conditions in New York and New England to see whether other reported cases of red spruce mortality might have occurred shortly after similar episodes of temperature anomaly. They discovered that two other documented periods of unusual red spruce mortality, one from 1871 to 1885, and the other from 1938 to 1945, also followed periods of unfavorable temperature extremes. Neither of those cases of spruce mortality lasted as long, or covered as much territory, as the present decline. However, they both occurred before the onset of severe air pollution in the Northeast.

No established physiological mechanism yet explained how or why late-summer/early-winter temperature extremes could trigger a decline of red spruce trees. Nevertheless, Johnson and the others believed it was possible that part of the current decline of the red spruce was attributable to this phenomenon. In an article that Johnson, Friedland, and Dushoff published in *Water, Air and Soil Pollution,* they concluded:

> Tree ring analyses suggest that red spruce are adversely affected by warm late-summer and cold early-winter temperatures. The timing of recorded episodes of red spruce mortality suggests . . . that climatic fluctuations have at least a synchronizing effect in the current episode of spruce decline and possibly in prior episodes of spruce decline. The mechanisms by which climatic events could cause spruce decline are speculative at present but might involve adverse effects of temperature on carbon budgets, and/or on winter hardiness.[13]

"Frost drought," "winter killing," "scorch," and "winter desiccation" are some of the names that botanists have given to a natural environmental stress that evergreens must deal with each winter. The most difficult time of winter for conifers in the Northeast is not during the long months of severe cold, but from mid-February to early spring, when temperatures can suddenly rise for a short time and when sunlight can become intense. On abnormally warm, sunny days in late February or March, the foliage and branches of evergreen trees receive strong solar radiation. Although the air remains cold and dry, the needles of the trees become very warm, causing the water stored in the foliage to evaporate at a faster rate than normal. Drying winds speed up the process of water loss. Water lost from this excess transpiration cannot always be fully replenished from the soil, because water movement is very limited in the winter when moisture in the soils and stems is frozen. This excess loss of water causes a drought condition in the trees until the ground thaws and soil moisture becomes available.

The needles of trees affected by the winter drying injury first turn yellow and then bright reddish-brown—in severe cases, whole stands of evergreens look as though they have been scorched by fire. The browning of the foliage is followed a few weeks later by the defoliation of the trees and the death of their branch tips and tops. The greatest damage usually occurs on trees with southern exposures to the sun and western exposures to the wind. Seedlings and saplings are often severely stricken, since most of their foliage is close to the surface of the snow, which effectively reflects the intense rays of the sun.

A small amount of winter injury occurs in northeastern evergreen forests nearly every year, but there have been a few instances when damage was severe. One of the worst cases was the winter of 1947 to 1948 in the Adirondack Mountains of New York. Weather conditions that winter set the stage for the tragedy that followed. October 1947 was the warmest and the fourth driest on record. It was followed by an especially cold winter, the coldest in twelve years. January and February 1948 brought an unusual number of bright, sunny days during which daily temperatures fluctuated from -35°F at night to 35°F during the day. These conditions were ideal for drying the foliage.

In an article published by the *Journal of Forestry,* two scientists from the U.S. Forest Service's Northeastern Forest Experimentation Station, Dr. John R. Curry and Dr. Thomas W. Church, Jr., reported the effect of that winter on the trees:

The first indication of winter injury appeared early in March 1948, when needles of many conifers showed excessive browning. Whole mountain sides were covered with these discolored trees ... heaviest damage occurring along northern margins of roadways, power lines, rivers, swamps, and similar exposed locations. Within a few weeks defoliation took place and the ground beneath the injured trees became covered with dead needles. The large numbers of brown and defoliated trees along the highways attracted public attention, and several newspapers and magazines commented on this condition.[14]

For three years following the winter of 1947 to 1948, Curry and Church studied the progress of the evergreen stands in the Adirondacks. They found that nearly half of all the conifers had suffered some amount of permanent injury, although in most cases the damage was light. As of February 1951, approximately two percent of the evergreens had died from their injuries and another eleven percent had at least one-quarter of their crowns killed by winter drying. The overall growth rate of the merchantable conifers was reduced by five percent for two years because of the injuries suffered during that severe winter.

The red spruces suffered greater losses than did the hemlocks, firs, pines, cedars, or other evergreen trees of the Adirondacks. This was primarily because the winter of 1947 to 1948 killed not only red spruce foliage but also a large percentage of the buds that would have begun to replace the lost foliage the following spring. According to Curry and Church:

One species, red spruce, showed extensive bud injury associated with initial needle injury and defoliation. Bud injury in this species was estimated to be roughly proportional to the extent of the defoliation. This type of injury resulted in death of twigs and branches and, in severe cases, the death of the trees. . . . Balsam fir suffered less bud injury and made better recovery than did red spruce.[15]

They concluded that red spruce was particularly susceptible to winter injury.

In 1979, Johnson began a five-year study of red spruce in Vermont to determine what role winter damage might be playing in the decline of the trees. He was joined later by three other scientists: Dr. Andrew J. Friedland from the University of Pennsylvania, Dr. Robert A. Gregory of the U.S. Forest Service's Northeastern Forest Experiment Station, and Dr. Lauri Kärenlampi from the University of Kuopio, Finland. Kärenlampi was engaged in a similar study on the effects of frost damage on Norway spruce in northern Finland. They observed hundred of vigorous and declining red spruces throughout the Green Mountains—on Camels Hump, Mt. Mansfield, Mt. Abraham, Texas Falls, Wolcott, and Bald Hill, Vermont. In the spring and summer of 1984, they took monthly photographs of selected branches from six red spruces growing at 3,300 feet on Camels Hump. They also took samples in April 1984 of browning 1983 needles for special study under a microscope.

Johnson and the others discovered that each year a number of red spruces lost some of their previous year's needles. In two of the five years, 1981 and 1984, the damage to foliage was especially severe. Weather records kept by the National Oceanic and Atmospheric Administration gave these scientists a clue to the cause. The longest and warmest winter thaws for the past ten years in Vermont had occurred during February 1981 and February 1984. Johnson and the others watched the trees most closely in 1984. They found that from late February through early March of 1984, trees of all sizes lost a large percentage of their 1983 foliage and buds; their needles turned reddish brown and then fell to the ground. The series of photographs taken that spring and summer confirmed that the discoloration and defoliation did not continue into the growing season, May through August.

In an article published in 1984 in the *Canadian Journal of Forest Research,* Johnson and the others reported that, in their opinion, winter damage was an important factor in the decline of the red spruce: "We suggest that the visual appearance of declining red spruce is consistent with winter damage as the major cause of foliar loss. . . . Our observations on the nature of foliar loss over the past five summers are consistent with the idea that repeated frost damage leads to the appearance of severe decline.''[16]

These scientists also addressed another question: Had winter damage triggered the decline of the red spruce, or merely contributed to a decline that had been set in motion by something else? By the end of 1984, there were only two plausible alternatives that could be precipitating the decline—winter damage and air pollution. Other natural environmental forces, namely adverse site conditions, natural-stand dynamics, long-term climatic change, and drought had been investigated by Siccama and Johnson and had been ruled out as likely or substantial factors in triggering the decline. Although one other natural condition, seasonal summer-winter temperature extremes, had not been ruled out, admittedly it was a speculative theory. If winter damage was also ruled out as a plausible explanation for what had triggered the decline, then there would currently be no viable alternative to the air pollution theory. The view of Vogelmann and Klein would be strengthened. On the other hand, if it could fairly be said that winter damage could have triggered the decline, then the argument could still be made that air pollution was nothing more than a minor contributing factor in the overall picture.

The answer Johnson, Friedland, Gregory, and Kärenlampi gave to this question was clear and concise: ``[W]e regard winter damage as a contributing stress in the latter stages of the red spruce decline syndrome.''[17] It could not fairly be said that winter damage had triggered the onset of the decline. Temperature records from the weather station on Mount Mansfield, Vermont, revealed that the periods of mid-winter thaw in the late 1950s and early 1960s were insufficient to trigger the extent of damage that the red spruces were suffering at the commencement of their decline.

Effects of Winter Damage on Trees. Source: USDA Forest Service.

There were good reasons to suspect that as a species red spruce was unusually susceptible to winter damage. Curry and Church had demonstrated that red spruces in the Adirondacks were more severely injured during the winter of 1947 to 1948 than any other species of evergreen tree. Nevertheless, red spruce trees had coped successfully with winters for eons, until the age of modern air pollution. Johnson, Friedland, Gregory and Kärenlampi considered whether air pollution itself could have made the trees more vulnerable to winter injury than normal. They found that it was theoretically possible.

Johnson and the others reviewed a number of factors that could explain why red spruce trees were suffering such serious winter injuries. They concluded that the explanation probably had to do with the ability of the trees to prepare themselves for winter. Major changes in metabolism occur in plants as they go through the stages of summer growth, winter dormancy, and the spring reactivation of photosynthesis. By the close of the growing season each fall, the complex process of cold acclimation must be complete. Starches must be converted to sugars, needles and shoots must be ripened and covered with the waxes that will protect them from drying winter conditions, and buds must be formed, set, and hardened. If all this is not finished by the time of the first severe freeze, the trees' needles, shoots and buds will be susceptible to serious injury.

Evergreens growing at high elevations do not have as much time to become winter hardy as do trees at the base of the mountains. The growing season is cooler and months shorter in the boreal zone than it is at low elevations. Spring comes sooner and autumn later in the valleys than on mountain tops. Scientific studies performed on Norway spruce in Austria, on Engelmann spruce in Wyoming, and on balsam fir in New Hampshire have all shown that year after year the needles of trees growing at the wind-exposed treeline were substantially shorter, had significantly less waxy coating, and lost much more water in winter than did the needles of lower-elevation trees of the same species and the same age. Therefore, the foliage of evergreens in the boreal zone is most susceptible to winter injury. Any new environmental stress that interferes with the ability of these trees to prepare their foliage for winter will make an already difficult situation worse.

The fact that the red spruce had been steadily declining in vigor for decades could explain why they were currently suffering an unusual amount of winter injury. If the overall health of a tree is reduced, it may not have the energy it needs to fully harden and develop its tissues. The series of photographs that Johnson and his colleagues took in 1984 showed that the development of needles from viable red spruce buds progressed normally during the growing season, but that the vigor with which they developed seemed to be subnormal in some instances. They concluded: "[I]t is plausible that the highly stressed trees are unable to fully harden and/or produce an adequate cuticle [waxy coating]."[18]

Since there were many stresses contributing to the overall decline of the red spruce, any one of them could be considered an indirect cause of the increased susceptibility to winter damage. Johnson and the others, however, discovered a direct pathway by which air pollution could be interfering with the growth processes that prepare a tree for winter.

For many years, scientists in Finland and elsewhere in high-elevation areas have been trying to improve the growth of spruce-fir forests by fertilizing them with nitrogen salts. Beginning in the late 1970s a number of these scientists, including Kärenlampi, discovered that the application of excessive amounts of inorganic nitrogen salts resulted in frost damage in spruce. The prevailing explanation was that the nitrogen caused the trees to continue growing later into autumn than normal, and that this delayed the process of winter hardening—by the time winter arrived, the tissues of the trees were still not adequately acclimated and developed for the cold.

The forests in the northeastern United States have never been intentionally fertilized, but they have been receiving excessive amounts of inorganic nitrogen compounds from polluted air for decades. The concentrations of nitrogen from nitric oxide, nitrogen dioxide, and nitric acid are greatest in the high-elevation boreal forests. The amounts of nitrogen in the foliage of the red spruce trees also increases with elevation. When Johnson, Friedland, Gregory, and Kärenlampi examined under a microscope the samples of damaged red spruce needles they had taken from Camels Hump, they found that many of them showed the same type of cell injuries that scientists in Finland had found in the damaged, heavily fertilized forests of northern Finland.

Johnson and the others summed up their conclusions in the *Canadian Journal of Forest Research:*

There is sufficient evidence to formulate a testable hypothesis with respect to the role of nitrogen in promoting a predisposition to winter damage. . . . It is conceivable that nitrogen supplied to foliage by cloud water and (or) to the soil by clouds and precipitation induces growth later into autumn and delays cuticularization of epidermis. If cuticle thickening is not optimum, and if starch to sugar conversions are not completed (Aronsson *et al.* 1976), the plants are more susceptible to damage from early frost or desiccation.[19]

Pole saws are used to cut branchlets from the crown to study the effects of drought on red spruces on Camels Hump and in other forests. Source: USDA Forest Service.

A scientist from Brookhaven National Laboratory, Dr. Lance S. Evans, decided to follow up on this "testable hypothesis". He also decided to expand the investigation of frost damage to include forests in the southern Appalachian Mountains where red spruce trees had recently been found dying in large numbers.

Dr. Evans took hundreds of foliage samples from high-elevation red spruces on Whiteface Mountain, New York, Clingman's Dome, Tennessee (the highest peak in the Great Smokies), and Mt. Mitchell, North Carolina (the highest mountain east of the Mississippi River). The samples were of foliage showing recent injury and the initial stages of dieback during the months of May and June 1985. He found the type of injury being inflicted on the trees to be remarkably similar at all three sites. During that early spring, red spruces on all the mountains simultaneously lost most of the needles of twigs that had elongated the year before. The symptoms he observed were similar to winter injury, and they were consistent with the observations Johnson had made on Camels Hump.

In an article published in 1986 by the *Canadian Journal of Forest Research,* Evans supported the theory that air pollution was predisposing the trees to winter desiccation they would not otherwise be suffering:

This common symptomology of recent injury of one species at high-elevation sites separated by great distances suggests that the stress factor(s) or causal agent(s) is not spatially localized. ... It is conceivable that materials such as nitrogen and sulfur in cloud water and other atmospheric depositions could alter normal frost hardiness of young, current-year shoots (Lovett *et al.* 1982). Possibly, the relatively high concentrations of nitrogen in cloud water could trigger excessive vegetative growth. This excessive vegetative growth could occur and override adequate cuticular development (DeLucia and Berlyn

1984), development of cold hardiness (Aronsson *et al.* 1976), and (or) bark development of current-year twigs to guard against winter desiccation injury. It is proposed herein that injury-causing apical dieback in red spruce at high elevations in North America is caused by inputs of materials from cloud water and (or) other types of atmospheric deposition that decreases frost hardiness (Friedland *et al.* 1984) and (or) bark formation in young twigs during the first overwintering period. . . .[20]

During the past thirteen years, the cumulative work of our most knowledgeable scientists has added a wealth of concrete data to the framework of understanding that Likens and Bormann began to assemble at Hubbard Brook from 1964 to 1974. Although there is now general agreement among scientists on many important aspects of the controversy over air pollution, substantial disagreement remains.

The consensus of scientific opinion is that the red spruces in the high-elevation forests of northeastern New England and New York are suffering widespread mortality and decline and that other species such as balsam fir are also losing ground in many locations. It is also agreed that the mountains in the Northeast are being subjected to extraordinarily high amounts of air pollution and acid precipitation. Most scientists concur that the devastation of the trees is probably caused by an environmental stress or combination of stresses.

Several logical pathways have been discovered by which air pollution could be stressing forest trees and causing the observed symptoms of death and decline. The majority of scientists have agreed that at least one form of air pollution, acid precipitation, is in fact stressing the forests and contributing to the overall decline of the trees. There is also a consensus among scientists that the synergy of stresses imposed on the forests by man-made air pollution could be the principal cause of the widespread destruction.

What scientists still disagree about is the degree of certainty with which the case against air pollution has been proven. Those skeptical of the air pollution theory point out that several documented episodes of unusual red spruce mortality have occurred in northern New York and New England since the early 1800s. Although most of these instances of unusual mortality were fairly localized, two were quite extensive. From 1871 to 1885, large numbers of dead and dying red spruce trees were reported throughout the region. Spruce beetle, drought, and temperature extremes were prevalent explanations offered at the time. By the late 1880s, estimates were that one-third to one-half of the mature red spruce timber forests in upper New York State had been killed; reports from Maine, New Hampshire, and Vermont suggest that losses of red spruce in those states were of similar magnitude. In the Adirondack Mountains, another documented period of unusual red spruce mortality commenced during the late 1930s and extended into the 1940s. Since these episodes predated the 1950s, they probably were triggered by a combination of natural causes alone. Thus, the argument goes, it is impossible to say with absolute scientific certainty that air pollution is a major factor in the current decline of the red spruce. These scientists have said that more study is needed to determine more precisely how much of the decline is attributable to air pollution as opposed to other causes.

No one claims that the air pollution theory has been proved with complete scientific certainty, but many U.S. scientists are convinced that the evidence generated to date is sufficient to prove to a high degree of probability that air pollution is playing a major role in the decline of the red spruce. To them, the evidence establishes to a high degree of scientific certainty that, in the absence of air pollution, the trees would not be dying. None of the earlier documented periods of red spruce decline was as extensive or long-lasting as the current decline. Therefore, these scientists argue, it cannot fairly be said that natural causes alone could have triggered and maintained such widespread destruction. Moveover, it will never be possible to prove with absolute certainty how much of the decline is attributable to air pollution alone, because no unpolluted spruce-fir forests exist to serve as experimental controls.

Scientists in Europe and Canada, who began their work on air pollution earlier than scientists in the United States, are virtually unanimous in the conclusion that air pollution is the cause of the widespread decline of the forests there. Despite years of costly research and debate, no one in the United States has been able to come forward with an alternative that can explain nearly as much as the air pollution theory does.

The best conclusion we can draw from the evidence generated by the ongoing scientific debate is that the tragic decline of the red spruce and other forest trees has probably been caused by a cast of interacting environmental stresses in which air pollution plays the key role. The severe environmental conditions that naturally exist on the mountains, together with adverse site conditions added by man-made air pollution, imposed enough stress on the high-elevation trees to predispose them to the possibility of widespread and serious injury. The continuing chronic levels of worsening air pollution, the acidification of precipitation in the 1950s, and to a lesser extent, natural stand dynamics together triggered the massive decline of trees no longer able to withstand the cumulative stress. The declining trees then became prey to other stresses that could not themselves have triggered such a decline in the absence of air pollution. Fungi, repeated winter damage, and periods of drought have contributed to the decline and magnified its intensity. Thirty more years of uncontrolled air pollution meanwhile has continued to contribute to the decline.

Using a diameter tape, member of a research team measures the d.b.h. of a red spruce on Camels Hump (d.b.h. is a diameter of a tree's girth taken at breast height, which is standard measurement at 4'3''). Source: USDA Forest Service.

6

Treatment Withheld

The most recent work of those scientists who study our nation's forests has produced a series of important discoveries that, unfortunately, have not received the attention they deserve outside the scientific literature. These discoveries elevate the issue of air pollution to a new level of national significance, and they call upon policymakers to reassess their views of both the cause for concern and the justification for action. The conclusion these discoveries suggest is that the federal government should immediately mandate substantial reductions in the emission of the atmospheric pollutants implicated in the decline of our forests.

Over the course of two decades of intensive research the scientific evidence linking air pollution with the decline of the forests has steadily accumulated. From 1964 to 1974, Likens and Bormann first documented the correlation between the decline of forests in the Northeast and the chronic levels of air pollution the forests were experiencing. During the next decade Vogelmann, Klein, and others proved that the correlation was no accident. Their work established several logical pathways by which a variety of air pollutants could be damaging the forests. They produced substantial evidence showing that the pollutants were in fact following those pathways and destroying trees. The most recent work by Siccama, Johnson, and others has shown that based upon evidence developed to date, natural causes alone probably could not have triggered and maintained the widespread decline. As the degree of scientific certainty has risen, the case for public action to reduce the implicated emissions has become stronger.

Recent discoveries have also revealed new reasons for concern over the cumulative effects of air pollution. As recently as 1980, it was generally believed that the problem of widespread forest decline was limited to northern New York and New England. However, with each passing year the territory of declining forests has expanded like the ever-widening circles of Likens' acid precipitation maps. From 1978 to 1981, Siccama, Johnson, and a number of their colleagues from the Yale School of Forestry and the University of Pennsylvania studied approximately 250 trees at 10 sites distributed throughout the Pine Barrens of southern New Jersey. The tree cores they took showed no major disruptions in the growth of the trees from 1852 to the mid-1950s. After 1955, however, two-thirds of the pitch pines, loblolly pines, and shortleaf pines in the study showed a sudden, abnormal and sustained decrease in growth rate. The decrease occurred in trees young and old, native and introduced; it showed up in trees of different species growing at different sites. A regression analysis of tree growth compared against 20 potential growth-limiting factors showed that the decline in growth correlated significantly with only one of the factors, the acidity of the stream water. They summed up their findings in an article published by the *Journal of Environmental Quality* in April, 1981:

> We investigated all of the obvious, plausible causes for the decreased growth rate. . . . However, the timing and uniqueness of the shift in growth patterns, the concomitant shift in factors related to growth, and the clear relationship between growth rate and stream pH indicate that acid rain merits strong consideration as a factor suppressing tree growth in the Pinelands.[1]

In March of the following year, another article appearing in the *Journal of Environmental Quality* reported that the same problem was occurring in the Shawangunk Mountains of southern New York.[2] Dr. L. J. Puckett, an ecologist with the U.S. Geological Survey found that eastern white pines, pitch pines, and chestnut oaks on the westerly slopes of the mountains had suffered a decrease in growth since the mid-1950s. After reviewing the various possible causes of the decline, he concluded that the most plausible explanation was

> . . . that acid rain and/or air pollution alone or in synergy with other growth-limiting factors has altered the relationship of tree growth to climate. . . . The implications of such a change pose several questions concerning future forest productivity and community structure. The added stress could possibly become great enough to significantly reduce annual growth rates of some tree species. Eventually, continuation of acid rain and air pollution could lead to the replacement of sensitive species by more tolerant species.[3]

In 1982 and 1983, there were reports of dying pines, spruces, and firs in Virginia, the Carolinas, and Tennessee. Some of the world's most magnificent wilderness areas, the George Washington National Forest, the Shenandoah National Park, the Blue Ridge Mountains, and the Great Smokies, were found to be suffering excessive conifer losses. Within a short period of time the syndrome of decline had spread to cover the full extent of the red spruce's limited range.

At locations from New Hampshire to Tennessee, mature eastern white pine trees were dying in unusual numbers. Eastern white pine is one of the East's trees most sensitive to damage by ozone. Ozone levels throughout the range of this species have proven to be high enough to cause damage to eastern white pine trees in the laboratory. The trees in the declining forests displayed the classical symptoms of ozone damage—changes in the size of the pine needles, yellowing and loss of needles, reduced availability of carbohydrates, decline in growth rate, loss of resilience, and death.

In 1982 and 1983, Dr. Harold S. Adams of the Dabney S. Lancaster Community College in Clifton Forge, Virginia, together with scientists from Fairmont State College in West Virginia and the renowned Oak Ridge National Laboratory in Tennessee, surveyed red spruce, balsam fir, and Fraser fir trees in Virginia and West Virginia to determine whether they were experiencing decline in growth similar to levels occurring in the Northeast. Cores taken from 258 trees at 10 different locations in both states showed an abrupt and substantial decline in the growth rates of the trees beginning after about 1965. The mid-1960s was a period of unusual drought in both states, but these scientists concluded, for two reasons, that it would be difficult to attribute the recent decline in growth rates of the trees to that drought period. First, there had been a drought of equal or greater intensity in Virginia and West Virginia around 1930, yet, the trees recovered quickly. Most of those same trees failed, however, to recover their growth rates after the drought of the 1960s. Second, although some of the red spruces cored in West Virginia did recover, they began to decline again in the 1970s.

In an article published in *Environmental and Experimental Botany,* these scientists concluded that air pollution had to be considered as a possible cause of the decline of these trees:

> . . . [T]here is some evidence that a pattern of decline in tree-growth rate has occurred in mid-Appalachian subalpine coniferous forests similar to that reported for several sites in the northern Appalachians. In comparable forests of New York, Vermont, and New Hampshire, the decline in growth rates observed for red spruce has been accompanied by extensive and widespread mortality. Whether or not this is now occurring or is likely to occur in mid-Appalachian forests has yet to be determined. However, it is certainly plausible that continuation of whatever stress is adversely affecting these forests would ultimately result in widespread mortality of both spruce and fir. If such is the case, long-term successional changes could occur involving replacement of these species by other species more tolerant of stress factors involved.[4]

More disturbing were the discoveries made on Mt. Mitchell in North Carolina, the highest peak east of the Mississippi River. In 1983 Dr. Robert Bruck, a plant pathologist from North Carolina State University, discovered that 90 to 95 percent of the red spruces and Fraser firs on the westerly slopes of Mt. Mitchell were dead or dying. Spruce trees there averaged 15 to 20 percent of their normal foliage. The visible symptoms of trees dying from the top down and from the outside in made the scene similar to, if not worse than, Camels Hump. Like Camels Hump, Mt. Mitchell was also subjected to chronic levels of nitric oxides, lead, and other airborne pollutants. When Bruck examined the roots of the trees, he found that they were black, and that they lacked fine feeder roots or helpful mycorrhizal fungi. There had been no drought there, and the one serious forest pest that Bruck found on Mt. Mitchell, an aphid, does not attack red spruce.

The geography of forests in decline continued to expand. In 1984, during a routine survey of the valuable commercial forests in the Piedmont regions of Alabama, Georgia, North Carolina, and South Carolina, the U.S. Forest Service reported an unexpected 20 to 25 percent decline in the growth rates of loblolly and shortleaf pines over the previous ten years. The Piedmont region has the highest average ozone concentrations for low elevations in the eastern United States. The decline in the growth rates of these conifers affected all ages and sizes of trees and was accompanied by increased mortality. This news was followed by the discovery that longleaf, loblolly, and slash pines in the eastern Coastal Plain of Florida were also affected. In an article appearing in the January 1987 issue of the *Journal of Forestry,* two analysts with the USDA Forest Service in Asheville, North Carolina, Dr. Raymond M. Sheffield and Noel D. Cost, reviewed the factors that could be contributing to the decline. Although many natural forces undoubtedly were at work, they could not explain all of the decline. Air pollution could not be excluded as a possible cause. They noted that "... scientific evidence can neither confirm nor refute whether atmospheric deposition has caused the reduction in pine tree and stand growth in the Southeast."[5] While scientists were investigating what role air pollution might play there, in August 1985 the U.S. Environmental Protection Agency (EPA) reported high acidity levels in 17 percent of lakes surveyed in Florida and southern Georgia.

Forest trees in the Midwest have not escaped significant air pollution stress. In the springs of 1979 and 1980, two scientists from the Institute of Ecology in Indianapolis, Indiana, Dr. Roland W. Usher and Dr. Wayne T. Williams, studied 373 eastern white pine trees growing at 13 locations throughout Indiana and Wisconsin. Some plots were in rural forests, others in urban settings. Similar amounts of ozone were measured in the air above all the study areas, although the nine sites in Indiana had more sulfur dioxide pollution than the four Wisconsin sites. Usher and Williams found symptoms of air pollution damage at all of the sites they visited. Although the trees in Wisconsin were much better off than their neighbors in Indiana, none of the rural sites was unaffected. In Indiana, 99.6 percent of the pines showed some sign of injury; more than half of the trees in Indiana had suffered significant damage to more than half of their needles. Of the trees in Indiana, 8 percent were "severely diseased."

Usher and Williams summarized their conclusions in an article they published in *Plant Disease* in March 1982:

Sufficiently high air pollution concentrations existed in rural and urban Indiana to cause extensive foliar injury to eastern white pine. O_3 and SO_2 were considered in this study to be the primary causal agents of the air pollution disease observed. Nitrogen oxides may also be interactive. . . . Continued stress from air pollutants on eastern white pine can be expected to cause changes in the ecosystem status of this forest species through depauperization of genotypes.[6]

This dire prediction proved true within a very few years. When scientists restudied the Indiana sites in 1984, they found that half the trees had died.

High levels of sulfur dioxide and ozone pollution emanating from the densely populated, industrialized Ohio River Valley have been implicated in the decline of several species of forest trees located not only close to major sources of the pollutants, but also within the more remote Hoosier National Forest. Sugar maple, red oak, white oak, white ash, and tulip poplar all showed signs of foliage damage and growth decline.

Forests in the western United States have not been immune to damage from modern air pollution either. Ponderosa pines in the San Bernardino and San Gabriel mountain ranges of southern California, located downwind of the Los Angeles Basin, have been in a state of decline since the early 1950s; ponderosa pine harvests there are down 80 percent since World War II. Scientists in California blame these phenomena on the extreme urban pollution emanating from nearby Los Angeles, and the frequent episodes of air stagnation in the area. Most scientists in the United States agree with the assessment that very high concentrations of ozone and other pollutants in the air have severely altered forest growth, mortality, and stand dynamics on those mountain ranges in the last few decades.

Beginning in the summer of 1974, Dr. Williams and a group of his colleagues began a long-term study of the Sierra Nevada Mountains to determine whether the problems in the San Bernardino Mountains were also to be found to the north in the magnificent forests of Sequoia National Park and King's Canyon National Park. Their study demonstrated that they were. Williams discovered that in 1974 air pollution damage to conifers was already common and extensive along the entire western slope foothills of the Sierra Nevada Mountain Range. Ponderosa pines, Jeffrey pines, giant sequoias, incense cedars, white firs, Lodgepole pines, and California black oaks all showed the classic signs of air pollution injury in Sequoia National Park and King's Canyon National Park. The symptoms of injury were identical to those observed in the San Bernardino National Forest. The most severely affected species were the commercially important ponderosa pines and Jeffrey pines. More than 70 percent of the trees at the study plots showed symptoms of injury. Trees growing in natural stands, managed stands, and plantations were all affected-even those growing at excellent sites. The pollutants that were causing the damage came from nearby Fresno and Sacramento in the San Joaquin Valley, and from as far away as San Francisco Bay.

In an article published by the *Journal of the Air Pollution Control Association* in March 1977, Williams and his colleagues concluded:

> In general, symptom intensity in the Sequoia area was lower than in the San Bernardino Mountains of southern California, but the distribution of symptom bearing trees was very extensive . . . A decrease in symptom severity was observed along an ordinate extending ridge by ridge eastward deep into the Sierras; this observation lends additional evidence to the long distance transport hypothesis. The present injury to the forest stands of the southern Sierra Nevada suggests that eventually the growth losses and mortality rates observed in the San Bernardino Mountains of southern California could develop in the survey area.[7]

Subsequent studies by Williams and by others have confirmed that the decline of those forests has continued to spread and intensify.

Through these disturbing developments, our forests are delivering a silent message. One major species of tree, the red spruce, is already being devastated throughout much of the range of its habitat. Unless action is taken to reduce some of the stresses that are overwhelming our forests, we can expect the destruction to continue, to intensify, and to claim more species of trees throughout more regions of the United States.

Our urban, industrial, and mobile society will inevitably bring with it a certain amount of air pollution. Concentrations of sulfur dioxide, nitric oxides, ozone, and heavy metals in the air are the result of industry, transportation, and electric generation, activities that affect the quality of our everyday lives. The quality of our lives, however, and our standard of living would be substantially reduced if we did not also have such precious natural resources as our forests. One of the primary goals of our public policy must be to control air pollution to the extent necessary to protect the integrity and health of our magnificent forests and parks, and this aspiration was embodied in the Clean Air Act of 1955. As presently enforced, however, the Act has failed to protect our forests from the ravages of excessive air pollution stress.

The forests in the United States are of inestimable value and economic importance. One of every three acres in this country is forested. More than 400 million of these forested acres are classified as commercial timberland, lands capable of producing greater than 20 cubic feet of industrial roundwood per acre per year, in natural stands. Nearly 75 percent of this commercial timberland is located in the eastern half of the United States, where air pollution stress is most severe. (See Figure 15.)

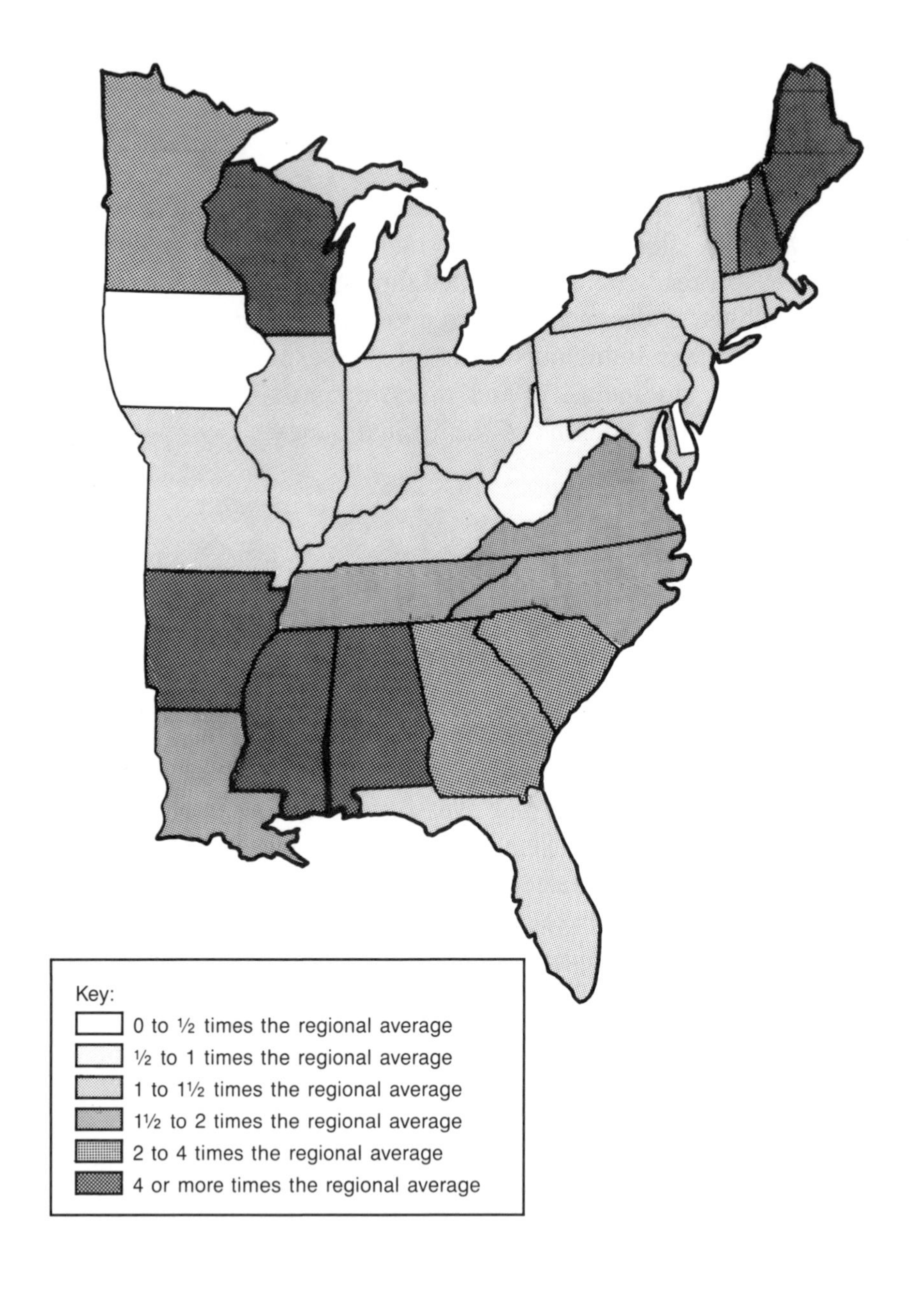

Fig. 15 — Forestry—Relative Economic Importance.

Relative importance of forestry-related income to State income, 1978-80. Source: Office of Technology Assessment, from U.S. Census Bureau data, 1984.

Most of the nation's forests are privately owned, but American taxpayers also have billions of dollars invested. As of September 30, 1982, there were more than 190 million federally owned acres in the National Forest System, and the federal government owned an additional 343 million acres of land devoted to wildlife, parks, and historic sites. Added to this are the tens of millions of acres of forest lands owned by the states and maintained as state forests and parks. The federal government recognizes that these priceless possessions are worth preserving, even at considerable expense. The U.S. Forest Service and the U.S. Park Service together spend hundreds of millions of tax dollars annually to protect our forests and parks from fire, insects, and disease to keep the forests beautiful and unspoiled.

The most important reasons for protecting the integrity and health of our forests are not economic or recreational. They are climatic and ecological. Dr. George H. Tomlinson II of Domtar, Inc., a research firm in Montreal, Canada explained this in an *Environmental Science & Technology* article published in June 1983:

Forests play an important role in many facets of life on this planet. They play a significant part in weather control by helping to preserve the hydrological balance between the atmosphere and the earth. Trees absorb, store, and, by transpiration from their foliage, slowly release water to the atmosphere. In the process, they reduce the deleterious effects of heavy rains and help to sustain atmospheric humidity in areas distant from the sea. In addition, forests contribute to the ecological balance between carbon dioxide and oxygen and store the sun's energy. Through the photosynthetic reaction that converts carbon dioxide and water to organic matter and oxygen, they provide part of the oxygen needed by most living organisms. . .. Aesthetically, the loss of forest over any substantial area, as in eastern Asia, has a devastating effect on the character of the landscape and consequently on the quality of life. Therefore, forest loss, whatever the cause, should be a matter of great concern.[8]

Since 1800 the world has destroyed 90 percent of its original forest base. Of the entire earth's surface, 55 percent is already classified as desert, and that figure increases every year. The shrinking of the forest base and the expansion of the desert regions are interrelated phenomena. In southeastern Mexico north of Veracruz, Vogelmann saw firsthand how the loss of a forest can turn a region into a bleak desert. In a paper published in *Natural History* in 1976, he reported:

> [E]ven during the dry season there is a great deal of moisture in the air, but it is in the form of fog. With the cutting of the forests, the farmers destroyed one of their most important sources of water—the moisture that the trees had combed from the fog.[9]

The drought that helped trigger the unprecedented famine in Ethiopia in 1985 has been blamed in part on the excessive deforestation that has been allowed to occur in Africa.

Despite the clear need to protect our forests from excessive air pollution stress, however, the federal government has failed to act in a meaningful way. The reason is that the EPA has not enforced the Clean Air Act in a way that would require polluters to reduce their emissions substantially. The Clean Air Act of 1955 tasks the EPA to promulgate air quality standards for air pollutants, requiring each state to bring the concentrations of air pollutants within its borders down to or below the EPA standards. The EPA, however, has not promulgated any standards for acid deposition, because it does not consider this to come within the Act's definition of "air pollution." The EPA has promulgated air quality standards for other pollutants, including sulfur dioxide, nitrogen dioxide, ozone and lead. However, current regulations can be satisfied by installing tall stacks, which convey pollutants to states hundreds of miles away from the point of origin. Similarly, dispersion techniques that emit high levels of pollutants during periods when weather conditions are likely to disperse those pollutants over a wide geographical area are also allowed. The one thing that the EPA has not required is the substantial reduction of total emissions.

In the mid-1970s, three federal appeals courts concluded that the agency's policy of relying upon dispersion techniques violated the Clean Air Act. The courts ruled that the Act allowed the use of such techniques only after the maximum degree of emission limitation achievable had been implemented.[10] The EPA Administrator, Russell E. Train, responded by issuing in 1976 a set of guidelines designed to promote reductions in emissions. Critics, however, charged that the guidelines contained a significant loophole—the use of tall stacks to meet air quality standards in cases where it would be economically unreasonable or technologically unsound to install the best available emission control technology. Congress, frustrated by the agency's continuing refusal to mandate emission reductions, enacted the Clean Air Act Amendments of August 1977. One of these amendments added a section to the Act that banned virtually all reliance on tall stacks and other dispersion techniques in achieving compliance with national air quality standards. Congress also directed the EPA to promulgate regulations to implement the amendments within six months.

The regulations due within six months were not finalized until February 8, 1982, four years later than the Congressional timetable required. By then administrations had changed twice, and Ann M. Gorsuch was Administrator of the EPA. Critics again charged that the agency's regulations were defective. Several states and environmental groups appealed the EPA regulations to the U.S. Court of Appeals for the District of Columbia Circuit. This delayed implementation of the 1977 amendments even further.

The Congressional Office of Technology Assessment (OTA) reviewed the agency's air quality standards to determine their long-term effects. In a report entitled *Acid Rain and Transported Air Pollutants,* OTA determined that the EPA standards "are expected to achieve reductions in total emissions within 30 to 50 years. Continuing emissions from both old and new sources, however, will maintain or increase pollution levels during the next few decades, unless additional controls are mandated."[11]

On October 11, 1983, the court held that the EPA regulations violated the Clean Air Act in a number of ways, and that they contained "arbitrary and capricious exercises of the discretion conferred on the EPA by the Act."[12] The Court of Appeals noted: "We have now passed the sixth anniversary of [the enactment of the 1977 Amendments]. During this time, polluters have not been obliged to reduce their emissions rather than rely on dispersion, because the statute must be implemented by the states, which have awaited EPA's regulations."[13] The court ordered the EPA to remedy the defects in its regulations within six months. Nevertheless, it took nearly two years for the Agency to issue new stack height regulations.

The new regulations, issued on June 27, 1985 by the EPA under its next Administrator, William D. Ruckelshaus, limited the number of "clean air credits" given to power plants and factories using tall smokestacks. Under the previous regulations, companies received credits because their tall stacks made the local air "clean." Under the new regulations, the credits were restricted to force companies either to switch to low sulfur coal or to install devices on their stacks to reduce the sulfur dioxide content of their emissions. The EPA estimated that the proposed regulations would reduce total sulfur dioxide emissions nationally by up to 1.7 million tons per year. Even if the regulations were to achieve that goal, the reduction in emissions would fall only 7 percent below current levels. The new regulations were immediately denounced as weak by environmental groups as well as by environmental specialists in Congress.

The regulation of tall stack emissions is not the only area where the EPA has failed to fulfill its mandates under the Clean Air Act. Section 126 of the Act authorizes any state to file a petition with the administrator of the EPA, if the state believes that facilities in other states are causing excessive air pollution to flow across its borders. The purpose of this provision is to achieve fairness among the states by preventing states downwind from becoming, in effect, dumping grounds for the air pollution emitted by other states. The law requires the EPA to hold public hearings on petitions filed under Section 126 and to issue a decision within sixty days. If the EPA finds that the claims of the petitioning state are true, then it has the power, under the Clean Air Act, to impose more stringent emissions controls on the offending facilities or to require them to cease operations until the violation is corrected.

On January 16, 1981, New York State filed a petition with the administrator of EPA, seeking relief for New York under Section 126 from air pollution originating in facilities in seven midwestern states. The petition stated that New York was prevented from attaining and maintaining national air quality standards for its citizens by pollution originating elsewhere. Further, this pollution interfered with state efforts to prevent significant deterioration of air quality within its borders. The states of Maine, Vermont, Rhode Island, Connecticut, Massachusetts, Pennsylvania, and New Hampshire joined in the petition, along with a number of environmental groups and individuals.

Since the petition was filed on January 16, 1981, Gorsuch was obligated to hold hearings and render a decision within 60 days, that is by March 17, 1981. She failed to do so. The petitioning states sued in federal court, seeking to compel EPA to respond to their petition. First Gorsuch and then Ruckelshaus, however, continued to refuse to issue a decision. On October 5, 1984, after nearly four years of delay, Judge Norma H. Johnson of the U.S. District Court for the District of Columbia, issued a decision stating that the Administrators had failed to perform their clear legal duty to act on the petition: "By creating the Section 126 petition process, Congress sought to establish a means of protecting citizens and the environment from the harmful effects of air pollution originating outside their home state. Defendant's delay in following his statutory mandate has compromised this process."[14]

Judge Johnson ordered a decision be made on the petition within sixty days from the court's action. On December 5, 1984, Ruckelshaus denied New York and the other states any relief from air pollution flowing from the midwest, citing ". . . the scientific and technological uncertainties which afflict this area of decision making."[15] The appeal, which was filed the next day, still awaited decision in early 1987.

Another example of EPA foot-dragging occurred in connection with emissions of nitrogen oxides and noxious particles from heavy duty vehicles and engines. The Clean Air Act Amendments of 1977 required the EPA to promulgate, by no later than the 1981 model year, standards that would require substantial reductions in the emission of nitrogen oxides from heavy-duty vehicles and trucks. The EPA was also required to promulgate by 1981 both maximum standards for the emission of noxious particles and conformance penalties to be imposed on manufacturers who failed to comply with the standards. Three administrators, successively, Douglas M. Costle, Gorsuch, and Ruckelshaus, did virtually nothing to comply with these requirements of the Act, except to make and break repeated promises that the required regulations would be issued "shortly." When the Natural Resources Defense

Council sued the EPA in federal court, Ruckelshaus requested another year within which to act.

Judge John H. Pratt of the U.S. District Court for the District of Columbia, refused EPA's request:

We find no reasonable ground for the delays thus far incurred . . . It is nothing short of astonishing that the agency seeks additional time to promulgate the required regulations when it offers not one shred of evidence as to why it has thus far failed to issue those standards.[16]

The court also castigated EPA for its inaction:

The EPA makes no showing of impossibility or infeasibility. It does not argue that it suffers from any staff or budgetary handicaps. Nor does it present any evidence of need for further study, technical or otherwise, of the major issues involved in [nitrogen oxide] and particulate emissions from heavy duty vehicles and engines . . . . Given the egregious delays encountered thus far, it is abundantly clear that a court order is necessary to make the EPA adhere to a definite regulatory schedule and execute its statutory duties.[17]

Judge Pratt concluded:

Defendant has had more than enough time to do the job Congress mapped out for it, and in light of the increasing evidence of health risks associated with [nitrogen oxide] and particulate emissions. . . we will tolerate no further delay in the promulgation of proposed and final regulations.[18]

The court issued an order accordingly, and the EPA complied. On March 15, 1985, the agency issued standards requiring reductions in nitrogen oxide and particulate emissions from heavy duty vehicles. Since, however, the Clean Air Act requires the EPA to give motor vehicle manufacturers a four-year lead time for complying with new nitrogen oxide emission standards, the EPA's long-overdue regulations for nitrogen oxide will not have any effect until the 1990 model year.

In spite of repeated reversals and repudiation in the courts, the EPA continues its refusal to pursue a federal policy on emissions reductions. In June 1985, the agency's current Administrator, Lee M. Thomas, unveiled a plan under which state and local governments, instead of the federal government, would handle air pollution problems applicable to their own geographical areas. Not surprisingly, many Senators and Representatives from the Northeast objected to the proposal. Attorney David D. Doniger of the Natural Resources Defense Council observed that EPA had "turned its long-standing failure to protect public health from passive neglect into deliberate policy."[19]

The EPA explains its refusal to mandate substantial reductions in emissions by saying that more research is needed to determine how large a role each of the implicated pollutants has played in the decline of our forests. Ruckelshaus' philosophy on acid rain can be summed up as follows: "If we act too quickly we may control the wrong pollutant."[20] His successor, Lee M. Thomas, has taken the same wait-and-see approach.

This approach, however, is based upon flawed assessments of the problem, of the benefits of more research, and of the risks of delay. It has been rejected by the overwhelming majority of the industrialized nations struggling to come to grips with the problem of air pollution. It also leaves the solution of a national problem up to the very states that may be causing the problem.

The claim that it would be unwise and unfair to regulate "the wrong pollutant" assumes that there is a "right" pollutant. It implies that there are many innocent suspects, but only one guilty pollutant whose identity has not yet been sufficiently established by the scientific community. This distorts the nature of the problem. The clear scientific evidence points out that each of the implicated pollutants can and does play a destructive role, and that the synergy of these stresses overwhelms the forests. The reason for mandating substantial reductions in all of the implicated pollutants is that they all share in the blame. Reductions in the emission of any one of them will help alleviate the totality of stresses that are ravaging our forests.

The EPA's policy assumes that additional research can produce more certainty about the causes and effects of air pollution. However, the complex nature of forest ecosystems makes this assumption highly questionable. Scientists who have devoted years of study to the impact of air pollution on forests advise that a greater degree of scientific certainty will be difficult to achieve. Natural forest ecosystems are so complex that there is rarely only one cause for an effect, or only one effect for a cause. Scherbatskoy put it succinctly in a paper he presented at the March 1984 Forestry Issues Conference held at Pennsylvania State University: "Given the inherent complexity of forest ecosystems, it is doubtful that we will ever fully understand all the variations in ecosystem response to environmental perturbation."[21] Even scientists who argue that there is no direct evidence that air pollution is to blame agree that research may very well be inconclusive. Dr. Allen S. Lefohn of Helena, Montana, and Dr. Robert W. Brocksen of the University of Wyoming acknowledged this in an article in October

1984 in the *Journal of the Air Pollution Control Association:*

> Over the next several years, the pace of acid rain research will be increasing. However, it is unclear whether the quality of the data produced from this increased pace will show a consonant increase. Increased federal spending is not necessarily synonymous with obtaining answers more quickly. The entropy of the universe tends to increase and with it, maximum randomness.[22]

As is often the case, the process of forging a scientific consensus becomes even more difficult when the subject is as politically controversial as air pollution. Spokespersons and scientists on all sides of the issue, including those engaged by special interest groups, trade data and arguments as the slow process of scientific validation continues. The pace of progress is itself fraught with danger to the forests.

The wait-and-see approach of the EPA rests upon a flawed assessment of the risks of delay. Put quite simply, when the stakes involve the integrity and health of our forests, we cannot afford to wait decades for a scientific breakthrough that may never come. Scientists have been telling us for fifteen years that unrelieved exposure to air pollution cannot but weaken the integrity and health of our forests. A forest ecosystem is a delicately balanced interaction between a large number of living components and environmental forces. No species of plant or animal exists in isolation. All forms of life, from the smallest fungus and moss to the greatest mammal and tree, support each other. If one component of an ecosystem is stressed or altered, other components will be harmed, and their responses will further shake the web of life.

Scientists have sometimes used stark language to make us focus on this fact of life. Likens and Bormann, 1972:

The early results clearly indicate that air pollution is an unpremeditated form of chemical warfare! Data collected on atmospheric pollutants and acid rain suggest a very serious problem in northern Europe. Existing data suggest that the problem in the United States, particularly in the Northeast, has already reached similar proportions. We urge consideration of these data in the establishment of air pollution standards.[23]

Vogelmann, 1982:

What seems to be overlooked in this controversy is that we need not, indeed cannot, wait until all the evidence is in before deciding if acidic precipitation affects plant or animal life. We need only recognize a few basic ecological principles which appear to have been lost in the furor of debate. These principles are like the Ten Commandments. People who follow them are unlikely to be led astray. Most important is: Every factor in the environment affects every other factor in the environment. The second is: If one factor is altered, many other factors will be altered.[24]

Dr. Samual B. McLaughlin of the Oak Ridge National Laboratory in Tennessee, 1983:

First, the perennial life form of forest trees makes chronic and potentially cumulative responses to stress likely. Secondly, the high species diversity of eastern deciduous forests enhances competitive interaction between species and increases the probabilities of competitive amplification or modulation of secondary stresses from air pollutants.[25]

Klein, 1984:

. . . (A)nthropogenically altered precipitation cannot fail to stress natural ecosystems. We must also remember that reductions in complexity of ecosystems by loss or pauperization of biota will reduce the stability of that ecosystem.[26]

With each passing year, as evidence of the intensifying and spreading forest decline has accumulated, these prophetic statements have proven to be increasingly true. The risks to our forests were real, especially in the montane boreal zones. There is now reason to fear that the red spruce may disappear altogether; there is serious doubt whether the tree can reverse its decline in the environment imposed on it. Siccama and Johnson in 1983 stated: "It is . . . important to determine whether a species can persist as an important component of forests after massive, synchronous mortality has affected all size and age classes."[27] Johnson, 1983: "Given the advanced state of spruce decline, it is unlikely that any measures could reverse the dieback/decline spiral."[28]

Vogelmann, Badger, Bliss, and Klein, 1985:

The evidence presented here . . . clearly demonstrates that red spruce decline on Camels Hump is real and is likely to be accelerating. For red spruce, the situation seems critical; most of the larger trees are devoid of needles, dead, and their tops have broken off. This can be seen not only on Camels Hump, but elsewhere in the Green Mountains (Jay Peak, Mt. Abraham, Bolton Mountain) as well as Whiteface Mountain in the Adirondacks (Scott *et al.* 1984) and southward in the Appalachians to North Carolina.[29]

Today, the future prospects for our forests are frightening many of our scientists. They fear that the damage we have seen on the tops of our mountains is just the tip of an iceberg.

According to Reiners, Marks and Vitousek, 1975:

Likens and Borman (1974) have suggested that technological

change, sometimes instituted in the interest of environmental quality, has converted local air pollution problems to regional problems. If this is a general trend, then it is likely that the hitherto protected high elevation environments will become the most exposed sites to certain pollutants. For this reason such ecosystems serve a special purpose as exposure monitors. In a sense, they are amplifying warning systems.[30]

Vogelmann, 1982:

But are trees in marginal environments the only vulnerable plants? Perhaps the dying spruces are the equivalent of the canary in the mine, a warning of imminent danger to trees that are now growing on more favorable sites. Accumulation of heavy metals and steady acid rains may eventually tip the balance of life, a balance that may be more delicately poised than we realize.[31]

Siccama and Johnson, 1983:

Particular attention has been given to the possibility that aluminum, a phytotoxic element mobilized in acidic forest soils by acid deposition, has induced effects on forest species. . . . Such effects would constitute a serious threat to the stability of forest ecosystems on acidic soils, both those that already show sign of decline and those that are still healthy . . . .[32]

Fortunately, our scientists have given us a prescription for avoiding disaster in the forests. Vogelmann and Klein, 1984:

It does not seem possible to us that the course and rate of terrestrial or aquatic ecosystem deterioration is capable of being slowed, stopped or reversed without very large reductions in the emission of acidic and metal-containing substances . . . Of course, additional information is required and will, in due course, become available.

The major question is, however, whether more than enough evidence is available now to permit the political and economic sectors to act. The peoples of the world have made much harder decisions and choices with much less evidence.[33]

Nineteen industrialized nations of the world have heeded the warning and advice of these scientists, and they rejected the EPA policy of inaction. They have concluded that the time has come to require substantial reductions in air pollution, because the risk of continuing damage is unacceptable. Austria, Belgium, Bulgaria, Canada, Czechoslovakia, Denmark, East Germany, Finland, France, Hungary, Italy, Liechtenstein, Luxembourg, the Netherlands, Norway, Sweden, Switzerland, the U.S.S.R., and West Germany have all committed themselves to reduce sulfur dioxide emissions by at least 30 percent by 1993, and to reduce other airborne pollutants, such as nitrogen oxides, as well. Some of those countries are only catching up to the United States in terms of air quality standards, but others are forging ahead of us. Nine of those countries have committed themselves to sulfur dioxide emission reductions of 50 percent or more by 1993. There are several clear parallels between the decline of the forests in the United States and decline of the forests in Canada and Europe. Our response to the crisis should also be in parallel.

The EPA failure to mandate immediate and substantial reduction of the implicated pollutants has resulted in leaving the solution of a national problem to the individual states. The very states that can solve the problem are the ones that cause it. There have been no signs, however, of a movement by heavily populated industrialized states towards voluntary emission reductions—nor should we expect them soon. Most of the states that produce most of the emissions have not only refused to go beyond EPA standards, but they have also actively opposed attempts to tighten the standards at the federal level.

Two states have moved to reduce emissions to lower levels than the EPA requires. Both did so out of enlightened self-interest to protect their own forests and resources from pollutants originating within their own borders. California has mandated the installation of special abatement devices on motor vehicle exhaust systems to reduce chronic ozone levels in the San Bernardino Mountains and elsewhere. On August 14, 1984, New York Governor Mario Cuomo signed into law statutes designed to reduce sulfur dioxide and nitrogen oxide emissions by power plants and other industries in the state by an estimated 12 percent by 1988, and 30 percent by the 1990s.

These actions by two states will help, but they are no substitute for a systematic national policy that can only be achieved by federal action. By pursuing its present course, the EPA is abdicating its responsibility to protect our national forests and parks from the ravages of air pollution.

The author exploring Camels Hump, Vermont. Source: Author's collection.

View of Camels Hump, Vermont. Source: Author's collection.

7

Twilight

Snowshoeing on Camels Hump in March can be easier than hiking the mountain in July. The snowpack underfoot covers the irregular contours of the trail with a smooth and even surface of glittering powder. Last night's contribution, another eighteen inches of new snow, buries the most treacherous patches of encrusted ice along the trail. It also coats the evergreens with wet, spring snow. Because of the weight of this snow, many of the small spruces and firs are bent over like monks in prayer. Occasionally, a branch or a tree is freed from some of its snowy burden by the wind or the warmth of the sun. When this happens, the tree suddenly springs upright again, sending a thundering cascade of snow to the ground and spurring a ruffed grouse into flight.

Each season the scene in this wonderful place changes, yet the relationships remain the same. In autumn and early winter, when the brown seeds of the red spruces fall with long wooden wings from the mature cones, pine siskins, crossbills, and red squirrels search them out for food. Pure stands of red spruce growing in close formation serve as winter cover for wildlife, and when the heavy snows of winter bury the feeding grounds of deer, rabbit and grouse, the animals eat the foliage and bark off the red spruce to survive until spring.

Man too has benefitted from these trees. Our ancestors discovered that the extracted essence of boiled red spruce twigs had valuable medicinal properties—it was a commonly-used antidote to the scurvy sailors often suffered on long voyages. From the early to mid-1800s a popular drink known as "spruce beer" was made by boiling the young branches of red spruces with flavoring and sugar. At the turn of the century, the chewing gum industry thrived on spruce gum, a forerunner of modern chewing gum made from chicle. Spruce gum made chiefly from the resin of red spruce trunks was harvested by gum pickers, itinerant workers who followed this industry during the winter months. Since the wood of the red spruce imparts no flavor, it was used in the nineteenth century to make butter tubs and boxes. The evenly grained, resonant wood of the red spruce has also been extensively used in the manufacture of violins, guitars, organ pipes, and piano sounding boards. The greatest use of the trees, however, was the extensive logging by paper and construction industries. The occasional abuses of excessive logging were always of serious concern. Then, in the 1950s, a new and more serious abuse, air pollution, began to show its impact.

Where I am today, on the Waterbury side of the mountain, not above 3,000 feet, there are no visible signs of the presence of man. This is a part of the Camels Hump State Park—a protected and remote area. But I now know that there is chemical evidence of man's invisible presence hidden in the heartwood of these trees. The few spruces in this spot, to which I have been coming for many years have not yet begun to show the visible signs of dieback and decline.

The need to regulate excessive air pollution has been recognized for at least seven hundred years, since 1285, when smog problems appeared in London because of the burning of soft coal. Laws were passed in an effort to limit the obnoxious odors and pollution, but people ignored them until 1306, when King Edward I made the burning of coal in London a criminal offense punishable by death.

The United States has often been at the forefront of efforts to preserve precious resources. Some of the greatest conservation movements in history began in this country. We have been blessed with resources that are the envy of the world, and with the wisdom to have preserved most of them at considerable expense. One example of the conservative approach was the decision to ban phosphate detergents to protect the Great Lakes from the "unproven" risk of harm, a decision that was of great value to the states in the Midwest. Our forests in the East are also an important part of our national heritage and economic foundation.

On the subject of controlling air pollution, however, the United States is falling behind, and a large part of the price we are paying for inaction can be found in the forests. On March 19, 1986, some hope came from the White House. The Reagan Administration had consistently refused to acknowledge that acid rain is caused by man-made air pollution or that it constitutes a serious environmental problem. The Administration's position had been that more study is needed before further federally mandated reductions in emissions would be warranted. On January 8, 1986, Drew Lewis, special envoy to Canada on acid rain, and his Canadian counterpart, William Davis, issued a joint report that implicitly rejected this position. The report found that "Clearly, man-made emissions of sulfur and nitrogen compounds contribute far more to acid rain in the United States than natural sources,"[1] and it called upon the U.S. Government and industry to spend a total of $5 billion over the next five years to develop technology for reducing sulfur dioxide emissions by burning coal more cleanly. Their conclusions came on the heels of similar pronouncements from the scientific community. The U.S. National Academy of Sciences issued reports in 1983, and again in March 1986, establishing a definite link between midwestern industrial sulfur emissions and environmental damage in the northeastern United States. The Academy of Sciences recommended that emissions be cut in half, a far more ambitious proposal than that put forward by Lewis and Davis. Nevertheless, the joint U.S.-Canadian report became a source of some hope for our forests when, on March 19, 1986, President Reagan publicly endorsed it. By doing so, he tacitly acknowledged for the first time that air pollution is a problem that requires federal action, not just study.

Another encouraging development occurred on April 10, 1986, when Rep. Henry A. Waxman of California introduced a new bill that, if passed, would require substantial reductions of national sulfur dioxide and nitrogen oxide emissions. The costs of compliance are estimated to be between $3.8 billion and $4.9 billion per year by the early 1990s. Although those figures appear to be large, the overall rise in electricity rates that would be required nationally to help fund the program would average only an estimated 2 to 3 percent. Representative Waxman's bill was co-sponsored by 150 other members of Congress.

Although these recent events are encouraging, they are not cause for celebration. President Reagan's endorsement of the Lewis-Davis joint report came in an important Congressional election year, after six years of unalterable opposition to substantial emission reductions. The Fiscal Year 1987 Budget presented by President Reagan on February 5, 1986, would *reduce* the EPA budget, rather than increase it by the recommended $1 billion per year. Moreover, the joint report itself does not offer any specific programs, goals, or timetables for the reduction of air pollution. It does not address the need to develop other techniques for reducing emissions besides the burning of coal more cleanly, and it is unlikely that a program funded at the level of $1 billion per year could effect substantial reductions. The Waxman bill could result in substantial progress if passed, but legislation has been offered in the House and Senate every year for the past five years without success.

The EPA, or Congress in its stead, should use these recent developments as an opportunity to review the most recent findings of our scientists, and to reassess its views of the nature of the problem, the benefits of more research, and the risks of further delay. If they do, they will find that the time has come to effect the immediate and substantial reduction of the two major pollutants that current technology can readily address, sulfur dioxide and the nitrogen oxides. The EPA and Congress will also find that the time has come to focus our research dollars on discovering new ways to reduce the other major pollutants—ozone, heavy metals, and acid precipitation—and to ameliorate the damage that has already been done. We cannot rely upon the courts to solve these problems. Although the courts have shown their willingness to take the EPA to task when appropriate, government by lawsuit on a case-by-case basis is no substitute for the comprehensive approach needed to address all the problems in a substantial way.

Even if we were to start this process today, it would take several years to fully implement a comprehensive program of control. Moreover, even after a comprehensive program is in place, the biological damage will undoubtedly continue for some years as the poisons already in the system work their way through. In the long term, however, not only will our forests benefit, but so will our lakes and streams, hundreds of which are already acidified and unable to support fish life. Our agricultural lands, which annually lose billions of dollars worth of crops because of air pollution, will also benefit. According to many scientists, the health of our citizens will be improved by reductions in these airborne pollutants. Furthermore, there will be less corrosion of our bridges, buildings, statues, and other structures.

In July of 1984, Klein and his wife, Dr. Deana T. Klein (Professor of Biology at St. Michael's College in Winooski, Vermont), presented a paper concerning acid rain, entitled "What's Happening To Our Forests?" at a symposium held at Gunnison, Colorado. They concluded their essay with the following observations:

But if our natural areas and our forest resources are to be retained—as we fervently insist they must—the immediate political and economic task is the one of reducing the pollutants, those in precipitations and those in the air. And we don't have forever to make up our collective minds. In particular sensitive areas containing especially sensitive species, it is likely that the next generation will experience very different forests than the ones that we now enjoy and use. Some of the effects appear to be irreversible—the demise of red spruce, for example—and no one knows what, if anything, will replace what has already been lost.[2]

The shadows of the trees are dark and long, transformed with the setting of the sun. Before leaving, I take one more glance at part of what could be the last stand of the red spruce.

Appendix 1

Historical Progress Toward Understanding Acid Precipitation*

Dates	Events
1661-2	Evelyn; Graunt; (England) noted the influence of industrial emissions on the health of plants and people, the transboundary exchange of pollutants between England and France, and suggested remedial measures, including placement of industry outside of towns and use of taller chimneys to spread the smoke into ''distant parts.''
1687	On the basis of experiments by Brotherton, Hooke (England) concluded that plants have ''two-fold kind of roots, one that branches and spreads into the earth, and another that spreads and shoots into the air; both kinds serve to receive and carry their proper nourishment to the body of the plant,'' wrote Hooke.
1727	Hales (England) noted that dew and rain ''contain salt, sulfur, etc. For the air is full of acid and sulfurous particles. . .
1734	Linné (Sweden) described a 500-year-old smelter at Falun, Sweden: ''. . .we felt a strong smell of sulfur. . . rising to the west of the city . . . a poisonous, pungent sulfur smoke, poisoning the air wide around . . .corroding the earth so that no herbs can grow around it.''
1852	Smith (England) analyzed the chemistry of rain near Manchester, England and noted concentric zones with ''three kinds of air—that with carbonate of ammonia in the fields at a distance, that with sulphate of ammonia in the suburbs, and that with sulfuric acid, or acid sulphate in the town.'' Smith also noted that sulfuric acid in town air caused fading in the color of textiles and corrosion of metals.

*Source: Cowling, E. B. 1982. Acid Precipitation in Historical Perspective. *Environmental Science & Technology (Series A)*. 16: pp. 111-117. Copyright 1982. American Chemical Society. Reprinted by permission.

Dates	Events
1854-6	Austria and Germany established "General Citizens Laws" prohibiting disposal of wastes by individuals on a neighbor's property. In the interest of encouraging industrialization, however, these same laws specifically excluded industries from legal liability when waste disposal caused pollution of water and air.
1855-6	Way (England) completed a very detailed series of analyses of nutrient substances in precipitation at Rothamsted Experiment Station and showed the value of these substances in crop production.
1872	Smith (England) published *Air and Rain: The Beginnings of a Chemical Climatology*, using for the first time the term acid rain and enunciating many of the ideas that we now consider part of the acid precipitation problem. These ideas included regional variation in precipitation chemistry as it is influenced by such factors as combustion of coal, decomposition of organic matter, wind direction, proximity to the sea, amount of rain, etc. After extensive field experiments, Smith proposed detailed procedures for the proper collection and chemical analysis of precipitation. He also noted acid rain damage to plants and materials and atmospheric deposition of arsenic, copper, and other metals in industrial regions.
1881	Brögger (Norway) observed "smudsig snefeld" (dirty snowfall) in Norway and attributed it to either a large town or an industrial district in Great Britain.
1909	Sørensen (Denmark) developed the pH scale to describe the acidity of aqueous solution.
1911	Crowther and Ruston (England) demonstrated gradients in acidity of precipitation decreasing from the center of Leeds, England; associated the acidity with combustion of coal; and showed that both natural rain and diluted sulfuric acid inhibited plant growth and seed germination, as well as ammonification, nitrification, and nitrogen fixation in soil.

Dates	Events
1919	Rusnov (Austria) demonstrated that deposition of substances from the atmosphere accelerated the acidification of both poorly-buffered and well-buffered forest soils.
1921	Dahl (Norway) recognized the relationship between acidity of surface water and trout production.
1922	Atkins (England) measured the alkalinity of surface waters and noted a relationship between alkalinity and biological productivity.
1923	MacIntyre and Young (U.S.) made the first detailed study of precipitation chemistry in the United States.
1925	Shutt and Hedley (Canada) made very early measurements of the nitrogen compounds present in rain and snow and commented on the value of these compounds for crop growth.
1926	Sunde (Norway) demonstrated the value of adding limestone to water in a fish hatchery.
1939	Erichsen-Jones (Sweden) demonstrated the relationship between acidity and the toxicity of aluminum to fish.
1939	Katz *et al.* (Canada) reported acidification and decreases in base saturation of soils caused by sulfur dioxide emissions from the lead-zinc smelter near Trail, British Columbia.
1939	Bottini (Italy) detected hydrochloric acid in precipitation near the volcano on Mount Vesuvius, thus demonstrating that there are natural sources of strong acids in precipitation.
1942	Conway (Ireland) completed the first modern review of precipitation chemistry.
1948	Egnér (Sweden) initiated the first large-scale precipitation chemistry network in Europe.

Dates	Events
1950-55	Eriksson (Sweden) enunciated in a general theory of biologeochemical circulation of matter through the atmosphere. He also expanded the regional network established by Egnér into the continent-wide European Air Chemistry Network, which has provided a continuing record of precipitation chemistry for three decades.
1953	Viro (Finland) developed a regional chemical budget by comparing analytical data for precipitation and river waters in Finland.
1953-8	Tamm (Sweden) demonstrated the great dependence of mosses on atmospheric sources of nutrients, especially nitrogen and expanded this concept to include most forest plants.
1953-5	Barrett and Brodin (Sweden), Parker and Gorham (England) and Houghton (U.S.) simultaneously investigated precipitation chemistry data for evidence of atmospheric acidity.
1954-61	Gorham (England) demonstrated that acidity in precipitation markedly influenced geological weathering processes and the chemistry of lake waters, bog waters, and soils; he demonstrated that hydrochloric acid from combustion of coal rich in chlorine predominated in urban precipitation whereas sulfuric acid predominated in rural precipitation; he established that acidity in precipitation affects the alkalinity and buffering capacity of lake and bog waters; and he established that the incidence of bronchitis in humans can be correlated with the acidity of precipitation.
1957	During the International Geophysical Year, a one-year study of precipitation chemistry was conducted in Europe, the U.S.S.R. and the U.S.
1958-9	Junge and Werby, Jordan, *et. al.* (United States) conducted the first regional studies of precipitation chemistry in the U.S. and noted the important of atmospheric sulfur as a source of nutrients for crops.

Dates	Events
1959	Dannevig (Norway) recognized the relationship between acid precipitation, acidity in surface waters and disappearance of fish.
1960-3	Gordon and Gorham (Canada) established that exposure to sulfur dioxide and resultant acid rain contributed to the deterioration of lake quality, vegetation, and soils near metal smelters.
1960-6	McCormick (U.S.) operated the first continent-wide precipitation chemistry network in North America for six years, showing that precipitation is generally acidic east but alkaline west of the Mississippi River.
1962	Carson (U.S.) simulated a global revolution in environmental awareness by publishing "Silent Spring" in which the term "poison rain" was used to describe concern about atmospheric transport and deposition of pollutants.
1967-8	Odén (Sweden) outlined the changing acidity of precipitation as a regional and temporal phenomenon in Europe; he used trajectory analysis of air masses to demonstrate that acidity in precipitation in Scandinavia was attributable largely to emissions of sulfur in England and central Europe; he demonstrated temporal trends in acidity and in the concentrations of major cations and anions in precipitation over various parts of Europe; he demonstrated the increasing acidity of Scandinavian rivers; he described biological uptake and ion-exchange processes by which natural acidification of soils would be accelerated by atmospheric deposition of ammonia and other cations; he postulated that acid precipitation would lead to displacement of nutrient cations, reduction in nitrogen fixation, and release of heavy metals (especially Hg) which would damage surface waters and groundwater; and he postulated acidity in precipitation as a probable cause of decline in fish populations, impoverishment of forest soils, decreased forest growth, increased disease in plants, and accelerated corrosion and other damage to materials.

Dates	Events
1970	Odén and Ahl (Sweden) discovered that soluble pollutants in snow accumulate in the snow pack and are released almost totally with the first meltwater in spring.
1970	Hultberg (Sweden) demonstrated the effect of acidity on fish populations in two Swedish lakes.
1971-2	Rodhe *et al.* (Sweden) developed the first quantitative analysis of long-distance transport of sulfur in Europe. Showed that distances of transport frequently exceeded 1,000 km., that the residence time of sulfur in the air is 24 days, and that fields of deposition are roughly symmetrical and slightly displaced to the northeast from sources of emission.
1972	Bolin *et al.* (Sweden) drafted Sweden's Case Study for the United Nations Conference on the Human Environment "Air Pollution Across National Boundaries: The Impact on the Environment of Sulfur in Air and Precipitation." They noted damage to materials as well as ecosystems caused by acid precipitation.
1972	Hvatum (Norway) demonstrated increasing content of lead near the surface of Norwegian peat bogs and postulated long-distance transport as the probable cause.
1972	Tyler (Sweden) reported heavy metal accumulation in forest soils and speculated about their probable effects on forest productivity.
1972	Granat (Sweden) described the temporal and spatial deposition of sulfate and acid over northern Europe.
1972	Jonsson and Sundberg (Sweden) established an experimental basis for the suspicion that acid precipitation had decreased the growth of forests in Sweden.
1972	Various agencies in Norway initiated the SNSF project, "Acid Precipitation: Effects on Forest and Fish."

Dates	Events
1972-80	Overrein (Norway) demonstrated accelerated loss of calcium and other cations from soils receiving acid precipitation; he also provided leadership for the SNSF Project from its founding in 1972 until its completion in 1980.
1972	Likens *et al.* (U.S.) discussed the regional distribution of acid precipitin and its significance for aquatic and terrestrial ecosystems in North America; and they indicated that nitric acid resulting from atmospheric transformation of NOx adds to theacidity of precipitation in the eastern U.S.
1972	Jensen and Snekvik (Norway) showed that acidity in lakes and streams caused major decreases in salmon and trout populations in Norway.
1972	Beamish and Harvey (Canada) reported decline in fish populations due to acidification of lake waters in Canada.
1972-80	Munshower, Huckabee, Blaylock and Tyler (Sweden) showed that mushrooms, mosses, and other vegetation in forests accumulate heavy metals, especially lead and cadmium. They found that wildlife feeding on these plants also accumulate the metals, sometimes making both the plants and the wildlife hazardous for human consumption.
1973	Malmer (Sweden) summarized research on the ecological effects of increasing sulfur deposition, especially with reference to Swedish conditions.
1973	Dickson *et al.* (Sweden) reported on the pH status of 314 takes in western Sweden.
1973	Wiklander (Sweden) proposed a general theory to account for the effects of acid precipitation on soil chemical properties.
1973-77	Ottar (Norway) led the Organization for Economic Cooperation and

Dates	Events
	Development in Europe in its continent-wide study of the long-range transport of air pollutants.
1974	Almer *et al.* (Sweden) summarized the effects of changing lake water acidity on fish populations in Sweden.
1974	Grahn *et al.* (Sweden) discovered that *Sphagnum* (peat moss) invades acidified lakes and streams inducing a self-accelerating oligotrophication of the water body.
1974	Cogbill and Likens (U.S.) published maps showing changes in acidity of precipitation in the eastern U.S. between 1955-56 and 1972-73.
1974	Hutchinson and Whitby (Canada) established that strongly acid rain near Sudbury, Ontario is accompanied by deposition and/or mobilization of heavy metals (especially nickel, copper, cobalt, iron, aluminum, and manganese). They found toxicity of these metals sufficient to inhibit germination and establishment of many native and agricultural species of plants.
1974	Shriner (U.S.) demonstrated that simulated rain acidified with sulfuric acid can accelerate erosion of protective waxes on leaves. They inhibit nodulation of leguminous plants, and alter host-pathogen interactions of plants.
1975	Brosset *et al.* (Sweden) described the chemical transformation and trajectories that lead to ''white episodes'' and ''black episodes'' of acid deposition in western Sweden. They showed that gaseous nitric acid increases acid deposition. And they established a state-of-the-art titration method for the determination of acidity in precipitation.
1975-82	Cowling (U.S.) testified in congressional hearings concerning the inadequacy of research in the U.S. on the ecological effects of acid precipitation. Together with many other scientists in the U.S. and Canada, he began the development of a permanent network to

Dates	Events
	monitor chemical changes in wet and dry deposition and to study their biological effects in various regions of the United States.
1975	Cragin (Greenland) determined the chemistry of precipitation in Greenland from 1300 to 1975 A.D. He found a continuing trend of increasing sulfate and lead concentration beginning about 1800 and rising even morerapidly after 1945.
1976	Schofield (U.S.) reported the results of lake surveys showing a decline in fish populations associated with acidification of lakes in the Adirondack Mountains of New York State.
1976	Kucera (Sweden) summarized evidence that acid precipitation accelerates the corrosion of metals.
1976	Summers and Whelpdale (Canada) summarized earlier studies of precipitation chemistry in Canada and identified northwest Alberta, southern Ontario, and Quebec, and the Atlantic Provinces as areas of present or potential impact by acid rain and snow.
1976	Leivistad and Muniz (Norway) documented a massive fish kill on the Tovedahl River associated with snow melting in the spring of 1975 and established that dead and dying fish had lost control of their blood salt balance.
1976	Tyler (Sweden) demonstrated that heavy metals in the litter layer of forests inhibit microbial processes, especially decomposition of organic matter.
1976	Galloway (U.S.), Berry (Canada), Granat (Sweden), developed standardized protocols for precipitation collectors and collection techniques.
1976	Hultberg and Grahn (Sweden) discovered a correlation between acidification of lakes and the mercury content of fish.

Dates	Events
1976	Pough (U.S.) showed that reproduction of salamanders is inhibited by acidity of surface waters.
1977	Hagström (Sweden) showed that reproduction of frogs is inhibited by acidity of surface waters.
1977	Rosenqvist (Norway) enunciated a general theory that acidification of soils and surface waters is due mainly to natural process in soils and to changes in patterns of land use.
1978	Greszta (Austria) demonstrated accumulation of heavy metals in forest soils leading to injury to young pine and spruce seedlings.
1978-80	Liljestrand and Morgan; McColl and Bush; Lewis and Grant; all showed that acid precipitation occurs in both urban and certain rural areas in the western U.S.
1979	Altshuller (U.S.) and McBean (Canada) documented the transboundary exchange of sulfur and nitrogen oxides between the U.S. and Canada.
1979	Odén (Sweden) showed by studies of surface waters in Sweden that acidification due to sulfur deposition had begun during the early 1900s.
1979	Liljestrand and Morgan (U.S.) completed a rigorous statistical analysis of trends in precipitation chemistry in the eastern and western U.S.
1979	Cronan and Schofield (U.S.) discovered that aluminum ions are leached by acid precipitation from soils into streams and lakes in concentrations toxic to fish.
1979	Galloway (U.S.) and Whelpdale (Canada) developed a new sulfur budget for eastern North America and showed that atmospheric sulfur in this region is predominantly of anthropogenic origin (about

Dates	Events
	95%) and that a substantial fraction (about 30%) of sulfur emissions in this region are deposited outside this region.
1979	Henriksen (Norway) developed a simple descriptive model for determining the extent to which acidification decreases the alkalinity of lake waters and applied this method to predict the vulnerability of lakes to acid deposition.
1979	Carter (U.S.) established a presidential initiative on acid rain, calling for a 10-year, $10 million-per-year interagency program of research on acid precipitation and its environmental consequences in the U.S.
1980	Huttburg and Wenblad (Sweden) discovered acidification of groundwater in western Sweden, postulated acid precipitation as the probable cause, established by surveys of 1,300 wells the frequency of heavy metal accumulation and plumbing problems associated with these wells.
1980	Abrahamsen (Norway) summarized many years of research on the effects of acid precipitation on forests and concluded that fertilization effects, particularly by atmospheric deposition of nitrogen, tend to offset nutrient leaching and other detrimental effects. Also emphasized that negative effects of atmospheric deposition on growth are most likely when nutrient deficiencies or imbalances are increased by acid deposition.
1980	Wetstone (U.S.) summarized the biological and materials damage of acid precipitation in relation to the pollution control laws in North America.
1980	Schindler *et al.* established an experimental system for controlled acidification of whole lakes; demonstrated that acidification eliminated organisms of several trophic levels at pH values as high as 5.8-6.0.; also demonstrated that microbial reduction of sulfate could partially protect lakes against acidification.

Dates	Events
1980	Ulrich *et al.* demonstrated a significant correlation between amount of soluble aluminum in forest soils, death of feeder roots in spruce, fir, and birch forests, and widespread decline in the growth of these forests.
1980	Drabløs and Tollan (U.S.) established an Integrated Lake Water Acidification Study (ILWAS), to determine detailed chemical budgets for H+, SO_4−−, NH_4−, NO_3−, Cl−, and other ions in three lake watersheds with differing degrees of acidification.
1981	Norton *et al.* demonstrated by analysis of lake sediments that increased depletion of soil nutrients and increased atmospheric deposition of lead and zinc in northern New England started prior to 1880.
1981	Rodhe, Crutzen, and Vanderpol (Sweden) developed a photochemical model for the formation of sulfuric and nitric acid during long-distance transport. The model shows that the transformation of both of these acids are coupled processes and that their transformation rates and distances of transport are influenced by hydrocarbons and various oxidants in the atmosphere.
1981	Rahn (U.S.) demonstrated that the Mn/V ratio of aerosols can be used as a tracer to determine the source-receptor relationships for acid deposition in North America.

Appendix 2

More Recent Developments on Acid Rain Recognized by National and International Agencies*

Dates	Agency Conclusion
1972	SO_2 and NO_X emissions are transformed in the atmosphere to sulfuric and nitric acid, transported great distances, and deposited on vegetation, soils, and surface waters. (United Nations Conference on the Human Environment Study).
1981	Acid rain has caused the destruction of "many species of fish and their prey." It has also caused toxic trace metals to reach concentrations in surface and ground waters that are "undesirable for human consumption." (National Academy of Sciences).
1981	Acid rain has led to "severe degradation of many aquatic ecosystems" in the United States, Canada, the United Kingdom, and Scandinavia. "Many thousands of lakes" have been affected. (National Academy of Sciences).
1981	Fish taken from acid waters show high concentrations of mercury and other heavy metals. (President's Council on Environmental Quality)
1981	The conditions that lead to the formation and long-range transport of acid rain are "reasonably well known." (National Commission on Air Quality).
1981	The circumstantial evidence relating power plant emissions to acid raid is "overwhelming." (National Academy of Sciences).

*Prepared by the National Commission on Air Quality for the Canadian Embassy, Washington, D.C., March 1985.

Dates	Agency Conclusion
1981	Between 75% and 90% of sulfate deposition in any state in the eastern half of the U.S. originates outside the state. (Atmospheric and Environment Research, Inc.)
1981	Provisions of the Clean Air Act that seek to control interstate pollution "have proved ineffective." (National Commission on Air Quality).
1981	A reduction in SO_2 and NO_X emissions should lessen acid deposition, improve visibility and help eliminate fine particles that are hazardous when inhaled. (National Commission on Air Quality).
1982	The waters and soils over "extensive areas of North America" are "susceptible to acidification." (Canada-U.S. Work Group 3A).
1983	Continued emissions of SO_2 or NO_X at "current or accelerated rates" pose clear evidence of "serious hazard to human health." (National Academy of Sciences).
1983	The emissions of SO_2 and NO_X in eastern North America are at least ten times larger from human activities than from natural processes. (U.S. Acid Rain Peer Review Panel).
1983	There is strong evidence for damaging effects onlimestone monuments, bridges and buildings, and other structures. (U.S. Acid Rain Peer Review Panel).
1983	There are numerous examples of streams and lakes in Canada and the United States that have experienced and are probably now experiencing depletion of alkalinity. (Canada-U.S. Work Group 1).
1983	The reduction in sulfur dioxide emissions is indeed the only way to stop the observed damage to lakes and streams. All other measures are costly local palliatives. (Canadian Peer Group Report).
1984	Efforts to reduce the long-range transport of sulfur emissions must

Dates	Agency Conclusion
	be "intensified" to "prevent damage to forests, soils, water bodies, ecosystems, crops and vegetation as well as materials including historical monuments." (Resolution adopted by 32 countries, Munich Conference).
1984	Although the Clean Air Act has reduced emissions of SO_2 since 1970, "this is not enough to deal responsibly with the ecological problems caused by acid deposition." (U.S. Acid Rain Peer Review Panel Report to the President's Science Advisor).

Endnotes

Chapter 1

Death in the Boreal Zone

1. Vogelmann, H. W. 1982. Catastrophe on Camels Hump. *Natural History.* 91 (November): pp. 8-14.
2. *Id.*, p. 8.
3. *Id.*
4. *Id.*

Chapter 2

Three Great Natural Enemies

1. Vogelmann, H. W. 1982. Catastrophe on Camels Hump. *Natural History.* 91 (November): p. 8.
2. Carey, A. C., E. A. Miller, G. T. Gemballe, P. M. Wargo, W. H. Smith, and T. G. Siccama. 1984. *Armillaria mellea* and Decline of Red Spruce. *Plant Disease.* 68: p. 795.

Chapter 3

A Close Correlation

1. Mook, P. V. and H. G. Eno. 1956. Relation of Heart Rots to Mortality of Red Spruce in The Green Mountain National Forest. For. Serv. Northeastern Forest Expt. Station Research Paper 59: p. 2.
2. Likens, G. E., F. H. Bormann, and N. M. Johnson. 1972. Acid Rain. *Environment.* 14 (March): p. 37.
3. Likens, G. E. and F. H. Bormann. 1974. Acid Rain: A Serious Regional Environmental Problem. *Science.* 184: p. 1176.

Chapter 3 Notes Cont'd

4. Whittaker, R. H., F. H. Bormann, G. E. Likens, and T. G. Siccama. 1974. The Hubbard Brook Ecosystem Study: Forest Biomass and Production. *Ecological Monographs.* 44: p. 253.

5. Vogelmann, H. W. 1982. Catastrophe on Camels Hump. *Natural History.* 91 (November): p. 8.

6. Quoted from Dumanoski, D. Killer Stalks the High Country. *The Boston Globe.* May 23, 1982, p. 75.

7. Siccama, T. G., M. Bliss, and H. W. Vogelmann. 1982. Decline of Red Spruce in the Green Mountains of Vermont. *Bulletin of the Torrey Botanical Club.* 109: p. 165.

8. Hilleman, B. 1982. Acid Deposition: Many New Findings in this Field Were Reported at the Recent Meeting of the American Chemical Society. *Environmental Science & Technology (Series A)* 16: p. 327.

Chapter 4

Discovering Invisible Pathways

1. Eaton, J. S., G. E. Likens, and F. H. Bormann. 1973. Throughfall and Stemflow Chemistry in a Northern Hardwoods Forest. *Journal of Ecology.* 61: p. 503.

2. Hutchinson, T. C. and L. M. Whitby. 1977. The Effects of Acid Rainfall and Heavy Metal Particulates on a Boreal Forest Ecosystem Near the Sudbury Smelting Region of Canada. *Water, Air, and Soil Pollution.* 7: p. 435.

3. Cronan, C. S. and C. L. Schofield. 1979. Aluminum Leaching Response to Acid Precipitation: Effects on High Elevation Watersheds in the Northeast. *Science.* 204: pp. 304-06.

4. *Id.*, p. 305.

5. Smith, W. H. and T. G. Siccama. 1981. The Hubbard Brook Ecosystem Study: Biogeochemistry of Lead in the Northern Hardwood Forest. *Journal of Environmental Quality.* 10: p. 328.

6. Moloney, K. A., L. J. Stratton,

Chapter 4 Notes Cont'd

and R. M. Klein. 1983. Effects of Simulated Acidic, Metal-Containing Precipitation on Coniferous Litter Decomposition. *Canadian Journal of Botany.* 61:p. 3341.

7. Tamm, C. O. 1976. Acid Precipitation: Biological Effects in Soil on a Forest Vegetation. *Ambio.* 5: pp. 235-8.

8. Klein, R. M. and H. W. Vogelmann. 1984. Current Status of Research in Acid Rain. Presented at the Technical Symposium on Acid Rain. Transport and Transformation Phenomena, the 1983 George D. Aiken Lecture Series, University of Vermont, Burlington, Vermont, pp. 5 and 10.

Chapter 5

The Search for Natural Causes

1. Johnson, A. H., and T. G. Siccama. 1983. Acid Deposition and Forest Decline. *Environmental Science & Technology (Series A).* 17: pp. 294-305.

2. Johnson, A. H., and T. G. Siccama. 1984. Decline of Red Spruce in the Northern Appalachians: Assessing the Possible Role of Acid Deposition. *Tappi Journal.* 67: pp. 68-72.

3. *Id.*, p. 72.

4. Johnson, A. H., and T. G. Siccama. 1983. Acid Deposition and Forest Decline. *Environmental Science & Technology (Series A).* 17: p. 298.

5. *Id.*, p. 303.

6. Johnson, A. H., and T. G. Siccama. 1984. Decline of Red Spruce in the Northern Appalachians; Assessing the Possible Role of Acid Deposition. *Tappi Journal.* 67: p. 70.

7. Johnson, A. H. 1983. Red Spruce Decline in the Northeastern U.S.: Hypotheses Regarding the Role of Acid Rain. *Journal of the Air Pollution Control Association.* 33: p. 1051.

8. Johnson, A. H. and T. G. Siccama. 1983. Acid Deposition and Forest Decline. *Environmental Science & Technology (Series A).* 17: p. 298.

9. Davis, M. B., and D. B. Botkin. 1985. Sensitivity of Cool-Temperate

Chapter 5 Notes Cont'd

Forests and their Fossil Pollen Record to Rapid Temperature Change. *Quaternary Research.* 23: pp. 335-6.

10. Johnson, A. H., and T. G. Siccama. 1983. Acid Deposition and Forest Decline. *Environmental Science & Technology (Series A).* 17: pp. 299-300.

11. Siccama, T. G., M. Bliss and H. W. Vogelmann. 1982. Decline of Red Spruce in the Green Mountains of Vermont. *Bulletin of the Torrey Botanical Club.* 109: p. 166.

12. Personal communication with the author.

13. Johnson, A. H., A. J. Friedland, and J. G. Dushoff. 1986. Recent and Historic Red Spruce Mortality: Evidence of Climatic Influence. *Water, Air and Soil Pollution.* 30: p. 327.

14. Curry, J. R., and T. W.Church, Jr. 1952. Observations on Winter Drying of Conifers in the Adirondacks. *Journal of Forestry.* 50 (February): p. 114.

15. *Id.*, p. 115.

16. Friedland, A. J., R. A. Gregory, L. Kärenlampi, and A. H. Johnson. 1984. Winter Damage to Foliage as a Factor in Red Spruce Decline. *Canadian Journal of Forest Research.* 14: p.964.

17. *Id.*

18. *Id.*

19. *Id.*, pp. 964-5.

20. Evans, L. S. 1986. Proposed Mechanisms of Initial Injury-Causing Apical Dieback in Red Spruce at High Elevations in Eastern North America. *Canadian Journal of Forest Research.* 16: p. 1115.

Chapter 6

Treatment Withheld

1. Johnson, A.J., T.G. Siccama, D. Wang, R. S. Turner and T. H. Barringer. 1981. Recent Changes in Patterns of Tree Growth Rate in the New Jersey Pinelands: A Possible Effect of Acid Rain. *Journal of Environmental Quality.* 10: pp. 429-30.

2. Puckett, L. J. 1982. Acid Rain, Air Pollution, and Tree Growth in Southeastern New York. *Journal of*

Chapter 6 Notes Cont'd

Environmental Quality 11: pp. 376-81.

3. *Id.*, pp. 379-80.

4. Adams, H. S., S. L. Stephenson, T. J. Blasin, and D. N. Duvick. 1985. Growth-Trend Declines of Spruce and Fir in the Mid-Appalachian Subalpine Forests. *Environmental and Experimental Botany.* 25: p. 323.

5. Sheffield, R. M. and N. D. Cost. 1987. Behind the Decline. *Journal of Forestry.* (January): p. 33.

6. Usher, R. W. and W. T. Williams. 1982. Pollution Toxicity to Eastern White Pine in Indiana and Wisconsin. *Plant Disease.* 66: p. 203.

7. Williams, W. T., M. Brady, and S. C. Willison. 1977. Air Pollution Damage to the Forests of the Sierra Nevada Mountains of California. *Journal of the Air Pollution Control Association.* 27: p. 232 and 234.

8. Tomlinson, G. H., II. 1983. Air Pollutants and Forest Decline. *Environmental Science & Technology (Series A).* 17: p.246.

9. Vogelmann, H. W. 1975. Rain-Making Forests. *Natural History.* 85 (March): p. 24.

10. *Natural Resources Defense Council, Inc.* v. *Environmental Protection Agency,* 489 F.2d 390,410 (5th Cir. 1974), *rev. in part on other grounds sub nom.; Train* v. *Natural Resources Defense Council, Inc.*, 421 U.S. 60 (1975). See to: *Big Rivers Electric Corp.* v. *EPA*. 523 F. 2d 16 (6th Cir. 1975) and *Kennecott Copper Corp.* v. *Train, 526 F. 2d 1149 (9th Cir. 1975),* cert. den. *96. S. Ct. 1665 (1976).*

11. *Acid Rain and Transported Air Pollutants: Implications for Public Policy.* (Washington, D. C.: U.S. Congress, Office of Technology Assessment, OTA-O-204, June, 1984), p. 105.

12. *Sierra Club, et al.* v. *Environmental Protection Agency,* 719 F. 2d 436, 439 (D.C. Cir. 1983).

13. *Id.*, pp. 469-70.

14. *New York* v *Ruckelshaus, E.R.C.* 1721, 1724, (D.C. Dist. 1984).

15. *49 Fed. Reg. No. 238*, p. 45154.

16. *Natural Resources Defense Council, Inc.* v. *Ruckelshaus,* 21 E.R.C. 1953, 1955, (D.C. Dist. 1984).

17. *Id.*, p. 1956.

18. *Id.*, p. 1957.

19. *Facts on File Yearbook.* 1985, p. 480.

20. See testimony of William D. Ruckelshaus before the Senate Committee on Environment and Public Works, on May 4, 1983 (on the occasion of his confirmation as Administrator of EPA), and on February 2, 1984 (on the subject of acid rain).

21. Scherbatskoy, T. 1984. Effects of Acidic Deposition in Forest

Chapter 6 Notes Cont'd

Ecosystems in the Green Mountains of Northern Vermont. *Proceedings of the Forestry Issues Conference.* Pennsylvania State University, March, p. 8.

22. Lefohn, A. S. and R. W. Brocksen. 1984. Acid Rain Effects Research—A Status Report. *Journal of the Air Pollution Control Association.* 34: p. 1011.

23. Likens, G. E., F. H. Bormann, and N. M. Johnson. 1972. Acid Rain. *Environment.* 14 (March): p. 40.

24. Vogelmann, H. W. 1982. Acid Precipitation: Should We Wait for Proof to Know When It's Raining? *Journal of Forestry.* 80: p. 563.

25. McLaughlin, S. B., T. J. Blasing, L. K. Mann, and P. N. Duvick. 1983. Effects of Acid Rain and Gaseous Pollutants on Forest Productivity: A Regional Scale Approach. *Journal of the Air Pollution Control Association.* 33: p. 1042.

26. Klein, R. M. 1984. Ecosystems Approach to the Acid Rain Problem. In *Direct and Indirect Effects of Acidic Deposition on Vegetation.* Ed. by R. A. Linthurst. Butterworth Publishers, Boston, p. 10.

27. Johnson, A. H. and T. G. Siccama. 1983. Acid Deposition and the Forest Decline. *Environmental Science & Technology (Series A).* 17: p. 303.

28. Johnson, A. H. 1983. Red Spruce Decline in the Northeastern U.S.: Hypotheses Regarding the Role of Acid Rain. *Journal of the Air Pollution Control Association.* 33: p. 1053.

29. Vogelmann, H. W., G. Badger, M. Bliss, and R. M. Klein. 1985. Forest Decline on Camels Hump, Vermont. *Bulletin of the Torrey Botanical Club.* 112: pp. 281-2.

30. Reiners, W. A., R. H. Marks, and P. M. Vitousek. 1975. Heavy Metals in Subalpine and Alpine Soils of New Hampshire. *Oikos.* 26: p. 273.

31. Vogelmann, H. W. Catastrophe on Camels Hump. 1982. *Natural History.* 91 (November): p. 12.

32. Johnson, A. H., and T. G. Siccama. 1983. Acid Deposition and the Forest Decline. *Environmental Science & Technology (Series A).* 17: p. 297.

33. Klein, R. M. and H. W. Vogelmann. 1984. Current Status of Research in Acid Rain. Presented at the *Technical Symposiumon Acid Rain: Transport and Transformation Phenomena,* the 1983 George D. Aiken Lecture Series, University of Vermont, Burlington, Vermont, p. 12.

Chapter 7

Twilight

1. Lewis, D. and Davis, W. 1986. *Joint Report of the Special Envoys on Acid Rain,* p. 10.

2. Klein, R. M. and D. T. Klein. 1984. What's Happening to Our Forests? Paper presented at the Ninth Annual Water Workshop: Acid Rain and the West: Direct and Indirect Effects. Western State College of Colorado, Gunnison, Colorado, p. 10.

Selected Bibliography

Chapter 1

Death in the Boreal Zone

Bormann, F. H., T. G. Siccama, G. E. Likens, and R. H. Whittaker. 1970. The Hubbard Brook Ecosystem Study: Composition and Dynamics of Tree Stratum. *Ecological Monographs* 40: 373-88.

Foster, J. R. and W. A. Reiners. 1983. Vegetation Patterns in a Virgin Subalpine Forest at Crawford Notch, White Mountains, New Hampshire. *Bulletin of the Torrey Botanical Club* 110: 141-53.

Hart, A. C. 1959. *Silvical Characteristics of Red Spruce*. U.S.D.A. For. Serv. Northeastern Forest Expt. Station Research Paper 124.

Rheinhardt, R. D. and S. W. Ware. 1984. The Vegetation of the Balsam Mountains of Southwest Virginia: A Phytosociological Study. *Bulletin of the Torrey Botanical Club* 111: 287-300.

Siccama, T. G. 1968. Altitudinal Distribution of Forest Vegetation in Relation to Soil and Climate on the Slopes of the Green Mountains. Ph.D. dissertation, University of Vermont, Burlington, Vermont.

Siccama, T. G. 1974. Vegetation, Soil and Climate on the Green Mountains of Vermont. *Ecological Monographs* 44: 325-49.

Stephenson, S. L. and H. S. Adams. 1984. The Spruce-Fir Forest on the Summit of Mount Rogers in Southwestern Virginia. *Bulletin of the Torrey Botanical Club* 111: 69-75.

Westvelt, M. 1953. Ecology and Silviculture of the Spruce-Fir Forests of Eastern North America. Journal of Forestry 51: 422-430.

Chapter 2

Three Great Natural Enemies

Harrington, T. C., D. M. Rizzo, and P. J. Marchand. 1984. Wind, Rocks, Root Disease and Mortality of Subalpine Red Spruce and Balsam Fir. *Phytopathology 74: 823 (Abstr.)*

Hepting, G. H. and M. E. Fowler. 1962. *Tree Diseases of Eastern Forests and Farm Woodlands.* U.S.D.A. For. Serv. Northeastern Forest Expt. Station Research Paper 254.

Houston, D. R. 1981. *Stress Triggered Tree Diseases, The Diebacks and Declines.* U.S.D.A. For. Serv. Report NE-INF-41-81.

Chapter 3

A Close Correlation

Budd, W. W. 1986. Trajectory Analysis of Acid Precipitation Data from the New Jersey Pine Barrens. *Atmospheric Environment* 20: 2301-06.

Cleveland, W. S., and T. E. Graedel. 1979. Photochemical Air Pollution in the Northeast United States. *Science.* 204:1273-1278.

Cogbill, C. V. 1976. The History and Character of Acid Precipitation in Eastern North America. *Water, Air, and Soil Pollution* 6: 407-13.

Cogbill, C. V., and G. E. Likens. 1974. Acid Precipitation in the Northeastern United States. *Water Resources Research* 10: 1133-37.

Cowling, E. B. 1982. Acid Precipitation in Historical Perspective. *Environmental Science & Technology (Series A)* 16: 110-23.

Eaton, J. S. and G. E. Likens. 1978. The Input of Gaseous and Particulate Sulfur to a Forest Ecosystem. *Tellus* 30: 546-51.

Fay, J. A., D. Golomb and S. Kumar. 1986. Modeling of the 1900-1980 Trend of Precipitation Acidity at Hubbard Brook, New Hampshire. *Atmospheric Environment* 20: 1825-28.

Galloway, J. N., G. E. Likens, and M. E. Hawley. 1984. Acid Precipitation: Natural Versus Anthropogenic Components. *Science* 226: 829-31.

Gschwandter, G., K. Gschwandter, K. Eldridge, C. Mann and D. Mobley. 1986. Historic Emissions of Sulfur and Nitrogen Oxides in the United States from 1900 to 1980. *Journal of The Air Pollution Control Association* 36: 139-49.

Hornbeck, J. W., and R. B. Smith. 1985. Documentation of Red Spruce Decline. *Canadian Journal of Forest Research* 15: 1199-1201.

Leedy, D. A. 1972. Fog Moisture Interception in the Green Mountains of Vermont. Master's thesis, Botany Department, University of Vermont, Burlington, Vermont.

Likens, G. E., and T. J. Butler, 1981. Recent Acidification of Precipitation in North America. *Atmospheric Environment* 15: 1103-9.

Lovett, G. M., W. A. Reiners, and R. K. Olson. 1982. Cloud Droplet Deposition in Subalpine Balsam Fir Forests: Hydrological and Chemical Inputs. *Science* 218: 1303-04.

Poirot, R. L. and P. R. Wishinski. 1986. Visibility, Sulfate and Air Mass History Associated with the Summertime Aerosol in Northern Vermont.

Atmospheric Environment 20: 1457-69.

Scherbatskoy, T., and M. Bliss. 1983. Occurrence of Acidic Rain and Cloud Water in High-Elevation Ecosystems in the Green Mountains of Vermont. *Transaction of the Air Pollution Control Association Specialty Conference*, The Meteorology of Acidic Deposition, Hartford, Connecticut, Oct. 16-19, 1983.

Stunder, B. J. B., J. L. Hefftner, and V. Dayan. 1986. Trajectory Analysis of Wet Deposition at Whiteface Mountain: A Sensitivity Study. *Atmospheric Environment* 20: 1691-95.

Vogelmann, H. W., G. Badger, M. Bliss, and R. M. Klein. 1985. Forest Decline on Camels Hump, Vermont. *Bulletin of the Torrey Botanical Club* 112: 274-87.

Vogelmann, H. W., T. Siccama, D. Leedy, and D. C. Ovitt. 1968. Precipitation from Fog Moisture in the Green Mountain of Vermont. *Ecology* 49: 1205-07.

Vukovich, F. M. and J. Fishman. 1986. The Climatology of Summertime O_3 and SO_2 (1977-1981). *Atmospheric Environment* 20: 2423-33.

Chapter 4

Discovering Invisible Pathways

Andresen, A. M., A. H. Johnson, and T. G. Siccama. 1980. Levels of Lead, Copper, and Zinc in the Forest Floor of the Northeastern United States. *Journal of Environmental Quality* 9: 293-96.

Baes, C. F., III, and S. B. McLaughlin. 1984. Trace Elements in Tree Rings: Evidence of Recent and Historical Air Pollution. *Science* 224: 494-97.

Cronan, C. S. 1980. Solution Chemistry of a New Hampshire Subalpine Ecosystem: A Biogeochemical Analysis. *Oikos* 34:272-81.

Cronan, C. S. and W. A. Reiners. 1983. Canopy Processing of Acidic Precipitation by Coniferous and Hardwood Forests in New England. *Oecologia* 59: 216-223.

Cronan, C. W., W. A. Reiners, R. L. Reynolds, and G. E. Lang. 1978. Forest Floor Leaching: Contributions from Mineral, Organic, and Carbonic Acids in New Hampshire Subalpine Forests. *Science* 200: 309-11.

Cumming, J. R., R. T. Eckert, and L. S. Evans. 1986. Effect of Aluminum on 32p Uptake and Translocation by Red Spruce Seedlings. *Canadian Journal of Forest Research* 16: 864-67.

David, M. D., and C. T. Driscoll. 1984. Aluminum Speciation and Equilibria in Soil Solutions of an Adirondack Mountain Forest Soil. *Geoderma* 33: 297-318.

Duchelle, S. F., J. M. Skelly, and B. I. Chevone. 1982. Oxidant Effects on Forest Tree Seedling Growth in the Appalachian Mountains. *Water, Air and Soil Pollution* 18: 363-73.

Friedland, A. J. and A. H. Johnson. 1985. Lead Distribution and Fluxes in a High-Elevation Forest in Northern Vermont. *Journal of Environmental Quality* 14: 332-36.

Friedland, A. J., A. H. Johnson, and T. G. Siccama. 1984. Trace Metal Content of the Forest Floor in the Green Mountains of Vermont: Spacial and Temporal Patterns. *Water, Air, and Soil Pollution* 21: 161-70.

Friedland, A. J., A. H. Johnson, and T. G. Siccama. 1986. Coniferous Litter Decomposition on Camels Hump, Vermont: A Review. *Canadian Journal of Botany* 64: 1349-54.

Friedland, A. J., A. H. Johnson, T. G. Siccama, and D. L. Mader. 1984. Trace Metal Profiles in the Forest Floor of New England. *Soil Science Society of America Journal* 48: 422-25.

Freedman, B. and T. C. Hutchinson. 1980. Long Term Effects of Smelter Pollution at Sudbury, Ontario, on Forest Community Composition. *Canadian Journal of Botany* 58: 2123-40.

Godbold, D. L. and A. Hüttermann. 1986. The Uptake and Toxicity of Mercury and Lead to Spruce (*Picea abies* Karst) Seedlings. *Water, Air, and Soil Pollution.* 31: 509-515.

Hutchinson, T. C., K. Bozic and G. Munoz-Vega. 1986. Responses of Five Species of Conifer Seedlings to Aluminum Stress. *Water, Air, and Soil Pollution.* 31: 283-94.

Johnson, A. H., D. G. Lord, and T. G. Siccama. 1982. Red Spruce Dieback in Vermont and New Hampshire: Is Acid Precipitation a Contributing Stress? *Acid Rain: A Water Resource Issue for the 80s.* Ed. by R. Herman and A. I. Johnson. American Water Resources Association, Bethesda, Md: 63-7.

Johnson, A. H., T. G. Siccama, and A. J. Friedland. 1982. Spatial and Temporal Patterns of Lead Accumulation in the Forest Floor in the Northeastern United States. *Journal of Environmental Quality* 11: 577-80.

Johnson, D. W., H. Van Miegroet, D. W. Cole, and D. D. Richter. 1983. Contributions of Acid Deposition and Natural Processes to Cation Leaching from Forest Soils: A Review. *Journal of the Air Pollution Control Association* 33: 1036-41.

Johnson, D. W. and D. D. Richter. 1984. Effects of Atmospheric Deposition on Forest Nutrient Cycles. *Tappi Journal* 67: 82-85.

Johnson, D. W., D. D. Richter, G. M. Lovett, and S. E. Lindberg. 1985. The

Effects of Atmospheric Deposition on Potassium, Calcium, and Magnesium Cycling in Two Deciduous Forests. *Canadian Journal of Forest Research* 15: 773-82.

Johnson, D. W., J. Turner, and J. M. Kelly. 1982. The Effects of Acid Rain on Forest Nutrient Status. *Water Resources Research* 18: 449-61.

Klein, R. M. 1984. Effect of Acidity and Metal Ions on Water Movement Through Red Spruce. *Acid Deposition: Environmental and Economic Impacts.* Ed. by D. Adams and W. Page. Plenum Publishing Co., New York.

Klein, R. M. and M. Bliss. 1983. Decline in Surface Coverage by Mosses on Camels Hump, Vermont: Possible Relationship to Acidic Deposition. *Bryologist* 87: 128-31.

Kress, L. W. and J. M. Skelly. 1982. Response of Several Eastern Forest Tree Species to Chronic Dose of Ozone and Nitrogen Dioxide. *Plant Disease* 66: 1149-52.

Like, D. E. and R. M. Klein. 1985. The Effect of Simulated Acid Rain on Nitrate and Ammonium Production in Soils from Three Ecosystems of Camels Hump Mountain, Vermont. *Soil Science* 140: 352-55.

Likens, G. E. and F. H. Bormann. 1974. Linkages Between Terrestrial and Aquatic Ecosystems. *BioScience* 24: 447-56.

Likens, G. E., F. H. Bormann, R. S. Pierce, J. S. Eaton, and N. M. Johnson. 1977. *Biochemistry of a Forested Ecosystem* New York: Springer-Verlag.

Lovett, G. M., S. E. Lindberg, D. D. Richter, and D. W. Johnson. 1985. The Effects of Acidic Deposition on Cation Leaching from Three Deciduous Forest Canopies. *Canadian Journal of Forest Research* 15: 1055-60.

MacLean, K. S. and R. G. Robertson. 1981. Trace Element Levels in Red Spruce and the Effect of Age, Crown and Seasonal Changes. *Communications in Soil Science and Plant Analysis* 12: 483-93.

McLaughlin, S. B., R. K. McConathy, D. Duvick, and L. K. Mann. 1982. Effects of Chronic Air Pollution Stress on Photosynthesis, Carbon Allocation, and Growth of White Pine Trees. *Forest Science* 28: 60-70.

Mollitor, A. V. and D. J. Raynal. 1982. Acid Precipitation and Ionic Movements in Adirondack Forest Soils. *Soil Science Society of America Journal* 46: 137-41.

Overrein, L. N. 1972. Sulphur Pollution Patterns Observed; Leaching of Calcium in Forest Soil Determined. *Ambio* 1: 145-7.

Reich, P. B., A. W. Schoettle, and R. G. Amundson. 1986. Effects of O_3 and Acidic Rain on Photosynthesis and Growth in Sugar Maple and Northern Red Oak Seedlings. *Environmental Pollution (Series A)* 40: 1-15.

Reich, P. B., A. W. Schoettle, H. F. Stroo, and R. G. Amundson. 1986. Acid

Rain and Ozone Influence Mycorrhizal Infection in Tree Seedlings. *Journal of the Air Pollution Control Association* 36: 724-26.
Reiners, W. A., R. H. Marks, and P. M. Vitousek. 1975. Heavy Metals in Subalpine and Alpine Soils of New Hampshire. *Oikos* 26: 264-75.
Richter, D. D., D. W. Johnson, and D. E. Todd. 1983. Atmospheric Sulfur Deposition, Neutralization, and Ion Leaching in Two Deciduous Forest Ecosystems. *Journal of Environmental Quality* 12: 263-70.
Ruhling, A. and G. Tyler. 1973. Heavy Metal Pollution and Decomposition of Spruce Needle Litter. *Oikos* 24: 402-16.
Scherbatskoy, T. 1982. Changes in Aluminum and Heavy Metal Concentrations in *Picea rubens* Wood in Northern Vermont. *Cambial Activities* Increment No. 7: 2-3.
Scherbatskoy, T. 1983. Responses of Spruce and Birch to Leaching by Acidic Precipitation. *Proceedings of the Fall Technical Meeting of the Northeast Atlantic International Section of the Air Pollution Control Association*, Durham,New Hampshire, Oct. 20.
Scherbatskoy, T. and R. M. Klein. 1983. Response of Spruce and Birch Foliage to Leaching by Acidic Mists. *Journal of Environmental Quality* 12: 189-95.
Schier, G. A. 1984. Response of Red Spruce and Balsam Fir Seedlings to Aluminum Toxicity of Nutrient Solutions. *Canadian Journal of Forest Research* 15: 29-33.
Scott, J. T., T. G. Siccama, A. H. Johnson, and A. R. Breisch. 1984. Decline of Red Spruce in the Adirondacks, New York. *Bulletin of the Torrey Botanical Club* 111: 438-44.
Siccama, T. G. and W. H. Smith. 1978. Lead Accumulation in a Northern Hardwood Forest. *Environmental Science & Technology* 12: 593-4.
Siccama, T. G., W. H. Smith, and D. C. Mader. 1980. Changes in Lead, Zinc, Copper, Dry Weight, and Organic Matter Content of the Forest Floor of White Pine Stands in Central Massachusetts Over 16 Years. *Environmental Science & Technology* 14: 54-56.
Tomlinson, G. H. II. 1985. Acid Deposition and the Loss of Nutrients from Forest Soils. *Tappi Journal* (March): 54-58.
Tukey, H. B., Jr. 1980. Some Effects of Rain and Mist on Plants with Implications for Acid Precipitation. *Effects of Acid Precipitation on Terrestrial Ecosystems.* Ed. by T. C.Hutchinson and M. Havas. Plenum Publishing Corp., New York.
Tyler, G. 1981. Leaching of Metals from the A-Horizon of a Spruce Forest Soil. *Water, Air, and Soil Pollution* 15: 353-69.
Ulrich, B., R. Mayer,and R. K. Khanna. 1980. Chemical Changes Due to Acid Precipitation in a Loess-Derived Soil in Central Europe. *Soil Science* 130: 193-99.

Vogelmann, H. W., G. Badger, M. Bliss, and R. M. Klein. 1985. Forest Decline on Camels Hump, Vermont. *Bulletin of the Torrey Botanical Club* 112: 274-87.

Whitby, L. M., and T. C. Hutchinson. 1974. Heavy Metal Pollution in the Sudbury Mining and Smelting Region of Canada. II. Soil Toxicity Tests. *Environmental Conservation* 1: 191.

Wood, T. and F. H. Bormann. 1974. The Effects of an Artificial Acid Mist Upon the Growth of *Betula Alleghaniensis Britt. Environmental Pollution* 7: 259-68.

Wood, T. and F. H. Bormann. 1975. Increases in Foliar Leaching Caused by Acidification of an Artificial Mist. *Ambio* 4: 169-71.

Zedler, B., R. Plarre, and G. M. Rothe. 1986. Impact of Atmospheric Pollution on the Protein and Amino Acid Metabolism of Spruce *Picea abies* Trees. *Environmental Pollution* 40: 193-212.

Chapter 5

The Search for Natural Causes

Aronsson, A., T. Ingestad, and L. G. Loof. 1976. Carbohydrate Metabolism and Frost Hardiness in Pine and Spruce Seedlings Grown at Different Photoperiods and Thermoperiods. *Physiologia Plantarum* 36: 127-32.

Baig, M. N. and W. Tranquillini. 1975. Studies on Upper Timberline: Morphology and Anatomy of Norway Spruce (*Picea abies*) and Stone Pine (*Pinus cembra*) Needles from Various Habitat Conditions. *Canadian Journal of Botany* 54: 1622-32.

Bormann, F. H. and G. E. Likens. 1979. Catastrophic Disturbance and the Steady State in Northern Hardwood Forests. *American Scientist* 67: 660-69.

Bormann, F. H., G. E. Likens, T. G. Siccama, R. S. Pierce, and J. S. Eaton. 1974. The Export of Nutrients and Recovery of Stable Conditions Following Deforestation at Hubbard Brook. *Ecological Monographs* 44: 255-77.

Conkey, L. E. 1986. Red Spruce Tree-Ring Widths and Densities in Eastern North America as Indicators of Past Climate. *Quaternary Research* 26: 232-43.

Delucia, E. H. and G. P. Berlyn. 1984. The Effect of Increasing Elevation of Leaf Cuticle Thickness and Cuticular Transpiration in Balsam Fir. *Canadian Journal of Botany* 62: 2423-31.

Fox, W. F. 1895. *The Adirondack Black Spruce.* Forest Commission, State of New York, Annual Report.

Harrington, T. C. 1986. Growth Decline of Wind Exposed Red Spruce and Balsam Fir in the White Mountains. *Canadian Journal of Forest Research* 16: 232-38.

Hornbeck, J. W., R. B. Smith, and C. A. Federer. 1986. Growth Decline in Red Spruce and Balsam Fir Relative to Natural Processes. *Water, Air, and Soil Pollution* 31: 425-30.

Houston, D. R. 1981. *Stress Triggered Tree Diseases, The Diebacks and Declines.* U.S.D.A. Forest Service Report NE-INF-41-81.

Johnson, A. H., D. G. Lord, and T. G. Siccama. 1982. Red Spruce Dieback in Vermont and New Hampshire: Is Acid Precipitation a Contributing Stress? *Acid Rain: A Water Resource Issue for the 80s.* Ed. by R. Herman and A. I. Johnson. American Water Resources Association, Bethesda, Md: 63-7.

Kerr, R. A. 1984. Climate Since the Ice Began to Melt. *Science* 226: 326-27.

Kerr, R. A. 1985. Wild String of Winters Confirmed. *Science* 227: 506.

Kincaid, D. T. and E. E. Lyons. 1981. Winter Water Relations of Red Spruce on Mount Monadnock, New Hampshire. *Ecology* 62:1155-62.

Lovett, G. M., W. A. Reiners, and R. K. Olson. 1982. Cloud Droplet Deposition in Subalpine Balsam Fir Forests: Hydrological and Chemical Inputs. *Science* 218: 1303-04.

Moloney, K. A. 1982. The Validity of the Concept of Climax in Relationship to Wave and Nonwave Areas of an *Abies balsamea* Forest on White Face Mountain, New York. Master's thesis, Botany Department, University of Vermont, Burlington, Vermont.

Nash, T. H., III, H. C. Fritts, and M. A. Stokes. 1975. A Technique for Examining Non-Climatic Variation in Widths of Annual Tree Rings with Special Reference to Air Pollution. *Tree-Ring Bulletin* 35: 14.

Scherbatskoy, T. and M. Bliss. 1983. Occurrence of Acidic Rain and Cloud Water in High-Elevation Ecosystems in the Green Mountains of Vermont. *Transactions of the Air Pollution Control Association Specialty Conference*, The Meterology of Acidic Deposition, Hartford, Connecticut, Oct. 16-19, 1983.

Soikkeli, S. 1978. Seasonal Changes in Mesophyll Ultrastructure of Needles of Norway Spruce (*Picea abies*). *Canadian Journal of Botany* 56: 1932-40.

Soikkeli, S. and L. Kärenlampi. 1984. The Effects of Nitrogen Fertilization on the Ultrastructure of Mesophyll Cells of Conifer Needles in Northern Finland. *European Journal of Forest Pathology* 14: 129-36.

Vogelmann, H. W. 1975. Rain-Making Forests. *Natural History* 85 (March): 22-25.

Vogelmann, H. W., T. Siccama, D. Leedy, and D. C. Ovitt. 1968. Precipitation from Fog Moisture in the Green Mountains of Vermont. *Ecology* 49: 1205-07.

Weetman, G. F. and R. M. Fournier. 1984. Ten-Year Growth and Nutrition Effects of a Straw Treatment and of Repeated Fertilization on Jack Pine. *Canadian Journal of Forest Research* 14: 416-23.

Wright, J. W. 1955. Species Crossability in Spruce in Relation to Distribution and Taxonomy. *Forest Science* 1: 319-49.

Chapter 6

Treatment Withheld

Bormann, F. H. 1976. An Inseparable Linkage: Conservation of Natural Ecosystems and the Conservation of Fossil Energy. *BioScience* 26: 754-60.

Bormann, F. H. 1982. The New England Landscape: Air Pollution Stress and Energy Policy. *Ambio* 11: 188-94.

Bormann, F. H. 1982. The Effects of Air Pollution on the New England Landscape. *Ambio* 11: 338-46.

Bormann, F. H. 1985. Air Pollution and Forests: An Ecosystem Perspective. *BioScience* 35: 434-41.

Bruck, R. I. and W. P. Robarge. 1985. "Observations of Boreal Montane Forest Decline in the Southern Appalachian Mountains—Soil and Vegetation Studies." North Carolina State University Acid Deposition Program, Dept. of Plant Pathology, Forestry and Soil Sciences, Raleigh, North Carolina.

Budd, W. W., A. H. Johnson, J. B. Huss, and R. S. Turner. 1981. Aluminum in Precipitation, Streams, and Shallow Groundwater in the Jew Jersey Pine Barrens. *Water Resources Research* 17: 1179-83.

Cogbill, C. V. 1977. The Effect of Acid Precipitation on Tree Growth in Eastern North America. *Water, Air, and Soil Pollution* 8: 89-93.

Graedel, T. E. and R. McGill. 1986. Degradation of Materials in the Atmosphere. *Environmental Science & Technology* 20: 1093-1100.

Hari, P., T. Raunemaa, and A. Hautojarvi. 1986. The Effects on Forest Growth of Air Pollution from Energy Production. *Atmospheric Environment* 20: 129-37.

Hinrichsen, D. 1986. Multiple Pollutants and Forest Decline. *Ambio* 15: 258-65.

Interagency Task Force on Acid Precipitation. 1982. *National Acid Precipitation Assessment Plan*. U.S. Government Printing Office #0-377-082/1146.

Interagency Task Force on Acid Precipitation. 1983. *Annual Report to the President and Congress.*

Johnson, A. H. 1986. Acid Deposition: Trends, Relationships, and Effects. *Environment* 28: (May): 6-39.

Kammerbauer. H., H. Selinger, R. Römmett, A. Ziegler Jöns, D. Knoppik, and B. Hock. 1986. Toxic Effects of Exhaust Emissions on Spruce *Picea abies* and Their Reduction by the Catalytic Converter. *Environmental Pollution (Series A)* 42:133-42.

Knight, H. A. 1987. The Pine Decline. *Journal of Forestry* (January): 25-28.

Likens, G. E. 1983. A Priority for Ecological Research. *Bulletin of the Ecological Society of America* 64: 234-43.

Linzol, S. N. 1986. Effects of Gaseous Pollutants on Forests in Eastern North America. *Water, Air, and Soil Pollution* 31:537-50.

Mayda, J. 1986. Forest Management and the Environment: Worldwide Trends in Legislation and Institutional Arrangements. *Forest Ecology and Management* 14: 241-57.

McLaughlin, S. B. 1985. Effects of Air Pollution on Forests: A Critical Review. *Journal of the Air Pollution Control Association* 35: 512-34.

McLaughlin, S. B., D. C. West, and T. J. Blasing. 1984. Measuring Effects of Air Pollution Stress on Forest Productivity. *Tappi Journal* 67: 74-80.

Miller, P. R., G. R. Longbotham, and C. R. Longbotham. 1983. Sensitivity of Selected Western Conifers to Ozone. *Plant Disease* 67: 1113-15.

Munn, R. E. 1986. An Integrated Approach to Assessing Acid Deposition. *Environment* 28 (May): 12-13.

Odum, E. P. 1985. Trends Expected in Stressed Ecosystems. *Bioscience* 35: 419-22.

Pinkerton, J. E. 1984. Acidic Deposition and Its Relationship to Forest Productivity. *Tappi Journal* 67: 36-9.

Prinz, B., W. H. Smith, E. B. Cowling, P. D. Manion, and S. B. McLaughlin. 1985. Prepared Discussion and Closing Remarks in Symposium Entitled: "Effects of Air Pollution on Forests: Critical Review Discussion Papers." Air Pollution Control Association. *Journal of the Air Pollution Control Association* 35: 913-24.

Rock, B. N., J. E. Vogelmann, D. L. Williams, A. F. Vogelmann, and T. Hoshizaki. 1986. Remote Detection of Forest Damage: Plant Responses to Stress May Have Spectral 'Signatures' That Could be Used to Map, Monitor, and Measure Forest Damage. *BioScience* 36: 439-45.

Rock, B. N., D. L. Williams, and J. E. Vogelmann. 1985. Field and Airborne Spectral Characterization of Suspected Acid Deposition Damage in Red Spruce (*Picea rubens*) from Vermont. *Proceedings of the 11th Interna-*

tional Symposium on Machine Processing of Remotely Sensed Data. Symposium, June 24-28,1985, Purdue University, West Lafayette, Indiana: 71-81.

Rosencranz, A. 1986. The Acid Rain Controversy in Europe and North America: A Political Analysis. *Ambio* 15: 47-51.

Rubin, E. S., M. A. Cushey, R. J. Marnicio, C. N. Bloyd, and J. F. Skea. 1986. Controlling Acid Deposition: The Role of FGD. *Environmental Science & Technology* 20: 960-69.

Smith, W. H. 1985. Forest Quality and Air Quality. *Journal of Forestry* 83: 82.

Turney, R. S., D. W. Wang, and A. H. Johnson. 1985. Biogeochemistry of Lead in the McDonalds Branch Watershed, New Jersey Pine Barrens. *Journal of Environmental Quality* 14: 305-14.

Vogelmann, H. W. 1973. Fog Precipitation in the Cloud Forests of Eastern Mexico. *BioScience* 23: 96-100.

Vogelmann, J. E. and B. N. Rock. 1986. Assessing Forest Decline in Coniferous Forests of Vermont Using NS-001 Thematic Mapper Simulator Data. *International Journal of Remote Sensing* 7: 1303-21.

Wang, D. and F. H. Bormann. 1986. Regional Tree Growth Reduction Due to Ambient Ozone: Evidence from Field Experiments. *Environmental Science & Technology* 20: 1122-25.

Williams, W. T. 1980. Air Pollution Disease in the California Forests: A Base Line for Smog Disease on Ponderosa and Jeffrey Pine in the Sequoia and Los Padres National Forests, California. *Environmental Science & Technology* 14: 179-82.

Williams, W. T. 1983. Tree Growth and Smog Disease in the Forests of California: Case History, Ponderosa Pine in *Series A* 30: 59-75.

Woodman, J. N. and E. B. Cowling. 1987. Airborne Chemicals and Forest Health. *Environmental Science & Technology* 21: 120-26.

Zedaker, S. M., D. M. Hyink, and D. W. Smith. 1987. Growth Declines in Red Spruce. *Journal of Forestry* (January): 34-36.

Chapter 7

Twilight

Hart, A. C. 1959. *Silvical Characteristics of Red Spruce.* U.S.D.A. For. Serv. Northeastern Forest Expt. Station Research Paper 124.

Westvelt, M. 1953. Ecology and Silviculture of the Spruce-Fir Forests of Eastern North America. *Journal of Forestry* 51: 422-430.

Index

L

M

N

V

W

Y

Z

ALSO AVAILABLE FROM ISLAND PRESS

Americans Outdoors: The Legacy, The Challenge
Report of The President's Commission on Americans Outdoors
Foreword by William K. Reilly

Here is the federal government's first attempt in more than 25 years to document fully America's need for expanded recreation facilities and opportunities. Its detailed analysis of recreation trends, patterns of use, and pressures on facilities ensure that this report will have a lasting impact and will be an important reference for anyone with a concern for how we can use and protect our recreation resources. The Island Press Edition is the only available volume that includes the full text of the Report, plus case studies showing how communities across the nation are addressing recreation needs; selected testimony; and a summary of key issues and recommendations prepared by the Commission.

1987. 426 pp., appendixes, case studies, charts.
Paper, ISBN 0-933280-36-X $24.95

Federal Lands: A Guide to Planning, Management, and State Revenues
by Sally K. Fairfax and Carolyn E. Yale

"This 252-page book made five file cabinets of documents, reports, and legal analyses obsolete."
—Dave Albersworth, Director, Public Lands and Energy, National Wildlife Federation.

The only comprehensive reference on the management and allocation of revenues from resources on public lands. *Federal Lands* outlines the legal history and details over twenty acts regulating natural resources. Discussion of fair market value; diligent development; below-cost timber sales; and preference rights leasing, and other key issues.

1987. 250 pp., charts, maps, bibliography, index.
Paper, ISBN 0-933280-33-5 $24.95

Green Fields Forever: The Conservation Tillage Revolution in America
By Charles E. Little, Foreword by Norman Berg

"As a farmer, I found Green Fields Forever a fascinating summation of tillage attitudes and a thought-provoking discussionof the erosion/chemical debate."
—Ralph Grossi, President, American Farmland Trust

Poor farming practices have been blamed for the soil erosion and decreased yields that have led to the current agricultural crisis. Conservation tillage has been offered as a solution, promising increased reliance on herbicides and pesticides, increased yields, and a chance for the land to renew itself. The several different variations of conservation tillage, including no-till, ridge-till, and strip-till are discussed. Little includes case studies of farmers who have actually used the various techniques.

1987. 192 pp., illustrations, appendixes, references.
Paper: $14.95 ISBN: 0-933280-34-3
Cloth: $24.95 ISBN: 0-933280-35-1

The Forest and the Trees: A Guide to Excellent Forestry
by Gordon Robinson, Introduction by Michael McCloskey

When is multiple-use multiple abuse? In this detailed look at the management of our forests, Gordon Robinson provides specific information on the principles of true multiple-use forestry and on what is wrong with forestry as it is practiced today. He describes, in practical terms, "excellent forestry"—uneven-aged management for sustained yield that safeguards the rich variety of life in the forest and protects all uses simultaneously. He offers the reader a short course in the mathematics of forestry and provides guidelines for commenting on forest plans. Includes nearly 400 summaries of published research and expert opinions. Gordon Robinson is a well-known and respected forester with fifty years experience in forest management.

1987. 288 pp., illustrations, tables.
Paper, ISBN 0-933280-40-8 $17.95
Cloth, ISBN 0-933280-41-6 $24.95

Tree Talk: The People and Politics of Timber
by Ray Raphael

"How can we provide the forest products we need on a sustained-yield basis? How can we extract timber from the woods while simultaneously preserving a healthy environment? How can we employ people in safe, stable, but personally challenging occupations within the forest products industry?" Ray Raphael asks these and other questions in this informative, balanced book on the production vs. protection debate surrounding our forests. This is a comprehensive look at the forest industry from the perspectives of environmentalists, loggers, old-time woodsmen, and young pioneers.

287 pp., glossary, references, illustrations, index.
Paper, ISBN 0-933280-10-6 $14.95

Land and Resource Planning in the National Forests
by Charles F. Wilkinson and H. Michael Anderson

This comprehensive, in-depth review and analysis of planning, policy, and law in the National Forest System is the standard reference source on the National Forest Management Act of 1976 (NFMA). This clearly-written, non-technical book offers an insightful analysis of the Fifty Year Plans and how to participate in and influence them.

1987. 400 pp., index.
Paper, ISBN 0-933280-38-6 $14.95

Pocket Flora of the Redwood Forest
by Dr. Rudolf W. Becking

This comprehensive field guide to the magnificent redwoods of the Pacific Coast—trees that are 2000 years old and reach a height of 350 feet—is interspersed with accurate drawings, color photographs, and systematic keys to plant identification. This superb collection, specially bound for outdoor use, is ideal for naturalists, students, teachers, and backpackers.

237 pp., drawings, photographs, index.
Paper, ISBN 0-933280-02-5 $15.00

Western Water Made Simple
By the Editors of *High Country News*

Winner of the 1986 George Polk Award for Environmental Reporting

"A miracle. The book lives up to its oxymoronic title—and then some. Fastpaced, full of the drama of high adventure, and comprehensive in its coverage, it is a triumph of journalistic lucidity and a stirring experience for the reader."
—Alvin M. Josephy, Jr., Author of *Indian Heritage of America*

This superbly organized, award-winning series of articles, now in book form for the first time, guides the reader through the most pressing issues affecting western water. By focusing on the West's three great rivers—the Colorado, the Columbia, and the Missouri—*Western Water Made Simple* presents a lively and penetrating account of the developments and controversies that must be understood by all those who are struggling to solve western development issues.

1987. 256 pp., illustrations.
Paper, ISBN 0-933280-39-4 $15.95

Public Opinion Polling: A Handbook for Public Interest and Citizen Advocacy Groups
by Celinda C. Lake with Pat Callbeck Harper, for Montana Alliance for Progressive Policy

"This handbook is an excellent, understandable guide to polling research. Whether you're working on a national campaign or a local city council race, this manual is an invaluable tool. It not only allows those on a limited budget to actually sample public opinion, but it helps everyone to better understand and critically analyze polls."
—Franklin Greer, campaign strategist

This book will not only help you plan and complete a professional poll, but also become a wise consumer of polls. This step-by-step guide helps to define the objectives the poll is intended to achieve, understand what a sample is, write questionnaires that get the information you want, conduct efficient interviews, and analyze and understand the results.

1987. 166 pp., bibliography, appendixes, index.
Paper, ISBN 0-933280-32-7 $19.95

Reforming the Forest Service
by Randal O'Toole

Is there support for below-cost timber sales? Is the Forest Service's goal to maximize its own budget—regardless of environmental considerations—rather than to maximize revenue from timber sales? Is the result excessive logging and clear-cutting? What reforms are necessary and how can the Forest Service be made more responsive and accountable to the public? Here is a provocative, in-depth examination of the Forest Service. O'Toole demonstrates economic inefficiencies and the environmental consequences of the laws that govern the agency. He proposes sweeping reforms that will make the Forest Service more environmentally sensitive and economically efficient.

1987. 250 pp., graphs, tables, notes.
Paper, ISBN 0-933280-45-9 $16.95

Breaking New Ground
by Gifford Pinchot, Introduction by George T. Frampton, Jr.

Conservation Classic

Today the Forest Service is in the midst of a crisis and surrounded by controversy. Gifford Pinchot, the first chief of the Forest Service, created our system of national forests and initiated the policy of multiple-use. *Breaking New Ground* expresses his vision of forestry in the United States and the responsibilities of the Forest Service. It offers a riveting, personal account of Pinchot's fight against private greed, bureaucratic corruption, and public indifference to create a system of long-range sustainable use. How has the Forest Service followed Pinchot's ethic since his death? In his introduction to the new Island Press Edition, George Frampton, President, The Wilderness Society, sheds light on the current controversy surrounding our national forests and the role of the Forest Service in protecting these natural resources.

1987. 542 pp., illustrations, index.
Paper, ISBN 09-33280-42-4 $19.95

These titles are available directly from Island Press, Box 7, Covelo, CA 95428. Please enclose $2.75 shipping and handling for the first book, and $1.25 for each additional book. California and Washington, D.C. residents add 6% sales tax. A catalog of current and forthcoming titles is available free of charge.